the GRIEF RECOVERY HANDBOOK *for* PET LOSS

the GRIEF RECOVERY HANDBOOK *for* PET LOSS

RUSSELL FRIEDMAN, COLE JAMES,
AND JOHN W. JAMES

TAYLOR TRADE PUBLISHING
Lanham • Boulder • New York • London

Published by Taylor Trade Publishing
An imprint of The Rowman & Littlefield Publishing Group, Inc.
4501 Forbes Boulevard, Suite 200, Lanham, Maryland 20706
www.rowman.com

16 Carlisle Street, London W1D 3BT, United Kingdom

Distributed by NATIONAL BOOK NETWORK

British Library Cataloguing in Publication Information Available

Library of Congress Cataloging-in-Publication Data

Friedman, Russell, author.
  The grief recovery handbook for pet loss / Russell Friedman, Cole James, and John W. James.
     pages cm
  ISBN 978-1-63076-014-4 (pbk. : alk. paper) 1. Pet loss. 2. Pets—Death. 3. Pet owners—Psychology. 4. Bereavement—Psychological aspects. 5. Adjustment (Psychology) 6. Human-animal relationships. I. James, Cole. II. James, John W., 1944– III. Title.
  SF422.86.F75 2014
  155.9'37—dc23

2014023262

♾™ The paper used in this publication meets the minimum requirements of American National Standard for Information Sciences—Permanence of Paper for Printed Library Materials, ANSI/NISO Z39.48-1992.

Printed in the United States of America

Dedication

First, we dedicate this book to all the grieving pet owners
who have received and returned the unconditional love of their pets.

We also dedicate this book to all the organizations that work
tirelessly to help the animals with whom we share our world.

As this book helps you regain a sense of
well-being after the death of your pet,
we hope you will feel compelled to make a
donation to the animal charity of your choice.

If you don't have a favorite charity, please consider
donating to one that's near and dear to our hearts:

Equine Outreach of Bend, OR
www.equineoutreach.com
541-419-4842

CONTENTS

INTRODUCTION

Millions of Pet Deaths Every Year—
But Very Little Effective Help

The death of pets affects people all over the world. In the
United States alone it is estimated that there are more than
14 million pet deaths each year. Death of a pet is an obvious,
heartbreaking loss. Pet loss can occur in many ways, including pets
that run away or are surrendered due to financial reasons. These
losses combined account for nearly 40 million new grievers every
year. Given the dimension of the problem, you'd think that there
would be a tremendous number of resources available for those
who have lost a beloved pet. But you would be wrong.

As you may have discovered, there is very little *effective* guidance for grieving pet owners. Yes, there are first-person books
in which grieving pet owners describe their pain, sometimes in
very poetic language. And yes, there are other books that provide some measure of comfort by helping the griever not feel
so alone. And yes, again, there are some support groups where
people can talk about the pain they feel in a safe nonjudgmental
environment. But those books and groups tend to provide only
short-term relief, not the kind of long-term completion of the
grief caused by the death of your pet.

Compounding the problem is the fact that friends—and even
family—often do not understand or accept the intensity of the
grief we feel when our pets die. That sad fact makes many pet
grievers isolate from human contact for fear they will be judged.

We have written this book to give you effective guidance in dealing with the death of your pet(s), whether that happened recently or a long time ago. We want you to be able to achieve a sense of completion, rather than resigning yourself to living with pain.

FUR, FEATHERS, FINS, SCALES, OR SHELLS

It's almost impossible to determine the exact origin of the human–animal bond. It probably began as a mutually beneficial hunting partnership. But the issue of blending skills in order to survive has long been trumped by an even more powerful link—the emotional bond—that ties us to our pets in ways that are sometimes hard to explain to those who just don't get it.

It may seem that dogs and cats are the focus of this book. But that's not entirely true. They are the central characters in this book because that reflects our personal experience to a large extent. But our emotional connections are not limited to furry canines or felines. Other body coverings may house the creatures we fall in love with—fur, feathers, fins and scales, or shells.

The bottom line is the heart line between us and another entity, and the degree to which it opens our own hearts. This book is for anyone and everyone who shares or has shared part of their life with a mammal, bird, reptile, fish, amphibian, or even an invertebrate. That covers all of the animal groups, from the commonplace to the exotic.

Many of us grew up with pets, but not every child had that opportunity. For a variety of reasons, some people don't get a pet until later in life. No matter when or why a pet comes into our life, we all retain the potential to forge a powerful emotional alliance. Others write eloquently about that emotional bond. But that bond is not the primary topic of this book.

The real topic of this book is what happens to us when that bond is severed by death, or disappearance, or even when circumstances force us to rehome our pets and we never get to see them again. Ultimately, the purpose of this book is to help you deal with the grief caused by the physical ending of your relationship with your pet.

ABOUT THE GRIEF RECOVERY INSTITUTE®— ITS FOUNDERS AND BOOKS

We are John W. James, Russell Friedman, and Cole James, and together we represent The Grief Recovery Institute. In the introductions to our other books, we mention that it's unlikely that a person would wake up one morning and say, "Grief, what a concept, I think I'll make it my life's work." That is not how it happened for John or Russell. Cole's story, as you'll read, is a little bit different.

Here is a brief outline of our lives, the institute, and the evolution of *The Grief Recovery Handbook* and our other books and articles.

John W. James is the founder of The Grief Recovery Institute and the original creator of the principles and actions of the Grief Recovery Method®. John did not choose the career of helping people deal with loss; it chose him—in a very painful way. In 1977, John and his then-wife had a three-day-old son die. Reeling from the impact of the death of his son, and then from the divorce that followed a few months later, John was forced to deal with the grief that brought him to his knees.

Trapped in pain and unable to get helpful guidance from friends, family, or professionals, John looked for a book that would tell him what he could do to deal with the pain in his heart; but the only books he was able to find were first-person recitations of the pain other grieving people had experienced. John didn't need to read about anyone else's pain, he had enough of his own. What he needed was a book that could answer this question: **"What can I do about it?"** (This is the same question grieving pet owners ask us.)

John couldn't find a book that answered that question, because at that time no such book existed.

John's Personal Recovery Created the Missing Book

Through trial and experimentation, John figured out a series of actions that helped him feel emotionally complete with his son who had died. It soon became obvious that his ability to help himself was valuable to others who were dealing with the death of children or other important people in their lives. John left his construction business and opened The Grief Recovery Institute. At that point, he realized that he could finally write the book he'd never been able to find—the one that answers the question, "What can I do about it?"

In 1986, John self-published the first edition of *The Grief Recovery Handbook*. Rather than being just another book that recites the pain of personal grief, it is a book of actions to help grieving people discover and complete what has been left emotionally unfinished by the death of someone important in their life.

When John began the odyssey that led him out of his emotional wilderness, he went back over all the losses that had affected his life. The first one he recalled was when he was six years old and his beloved dog, Peggy, died. The day she died, John's parents said, "Don't feel bad, on Saturday we'll get you a new dog." But John did feel bad, and he didn't want another dog. That incorrect information, from his parents, who were powerful authority sources to John, negated his normal and natural emotional reaction to the loss and set up the false idea that relationships can simply be replaced like light bulbs.

The story about Peggy's death, and John's parents' guidance, is the cornerstone of the misinformation in the original edition of *The Grief Recovery Handbook*, and in all subsequent editions. As you will see, it is also a major part of the foundation of this book to help you look at many of the ideas you may have learned about grief to see if they are valuable and helpful for you. If not, we'll help you discard them and teach you better ways to deal with your grief.

In 1988, Harper & Row published an updated version of *The Grief Recovery Handbook*, written by John and coauthor Frank Cherry. In 1998, HarperCollins published the revised edition written by John and Russell Friedman. And in 2009, HarperCollins published the 20th anniversary expanded edition, also by John and Russell.

Russell Friedman joined John at The Grief Recovery Institute as a volunteer in 1987. He arrived on the heels of his second divorce and a major financial meltdown that led to bankruptcy. Devastated by that one-two punch of losses, he was having a very difficult time with the emotional roller coaster that had become his day-to-day life. Like John, Russell also feels that he didn't choose a career in grief recovery, but that it chose him. The circumstances that led him to show up at the institute were totally random, as was the impulse to call John and volunteer the day after attending an event where John was the featured speaker.

Here's Russell's version of how it happened: "The day after the presentation, I was sitting in my apartment in Hollywood; my car had already been repossessed. As I sat there trying to figure what to do with the rest of my life, I spotted John's business card, which I'd gotten at the event. I decided to call him to thank him. After John answered the phone, I mentioned that I had been at the event the day before and I wanted to thank him. He said 'You're welcome.' There was a pause, and then my mouth opened and a voice came out of it and said, 'I want to volunteer to work for you.' I looked around my apartment and I was the only one there, so it had been me who'd said that. John was quiet on the other end of the phone for a bit and then he said, 'Well, can you come to the office tomorrow, and we'll talk?' Luckily the office was only a few blocks from my apartment so I was able to walk. I went up there the next day, and we talked. The following day, I began working at the institute as a volunteer. I've been there ever since."

Of course, when John tells the same story, or at least his side of it, it's a whole lot simpler and shorter. He just says, "Russell came up to the office one day twenty-seven years ago, and he hasn't left yet. So we became partners, coauthors, and friends."

As for **Cole James**, if you guessed that John W. James and Cole James are related, you'd be right. We'll let Cole tell you the story of how and why he is one of the coauthors of this book:

My name is Cole James and I work at The Grief Recovery Institute. I am a Certified Grief Recovery Specialist®. My father, John W. James, founded the institute, and I will forever be in awe of what he did for the world. I've cheered for my dad and Russell from the sidelines for as long as I can remember.

I never thought of working at the institute—I had other plans for what I was going to do with my life. That was until grief went from theoretical to personal for me. By my midtwenties, I had lost a friend to drunk driving, a cousin to suicide, and all of my grandparents. Last but not least, I'd said my final good-byes to three dogs and one cat.

I was enjoying a successful career working in television when I attended a four-day Grief Recovery Method Certification training. I went partly to see exactly what my dad did, and also because I knew I had some losses that were accumulating in my tummy and they didn't feel good.

That weekend changed the trajectory of my life. It was so powerful that I couldn't understand why this information wasn't available to everyone. I wanted to help spread the message in any way I could. At the end of that four-day training I made plans to give notice at my job and join The Grief Recovery Institute full time. I'm pretty sure that all of my entertainment industry colleagues thought I was crazy when I told them. "You're doing what?" "That sounds so depressing."

I have been on board now for four years, and I can tell you this work is anything but depressing. It is uplifting. The feeling I get when I've been able to guide people to release the pain they've been carrying around is indescribable.

Because I've had such close relationships with animals my whole life, and because I've had to deal with my grief when they died, I was thrilled when my dad and Russell asked me to coauthor this book. Along with many other amazing events over the past four years, it's proof positive that the decision I made to join the institute was the right one for me.

ADDITIONAL CONTRIBUTORS TO THIS BOOK

Derek Cooke: We are honored to introduce you to our very dear and long-term friend, Derek Cooke, of Abbey Glen Pet Memorial Park (www.abbeyglen.com). Derek has been in the forefront of creating awareness about the dignified handling of our pets' remains, the importance of conclusionary rituals and memorializing our pets, and for fostering emotionally respectful interactions with grieving pet owners.

Derek has written a powerful chapter of this book that will help you understand more about pet memorials, disposition of remains, and other important issues that will help you make choices that might otherwise be daunting, since they are often made at a time of emotional crisis.

Carole Batchelor: Carole is our partner and the director of the Grief Recovery Method in the United Kingdom (http://www.griefrecoverymethod.co.uk/).

Nick Ricketts: Nick is a new friend and chairman of the Association of Private Pet Cemeteries and Crematoria (http://www.appcc.org.uk/).

Together, Carole and Nick have given even more substance to the chapter on conclusionary rituals—adding awareness about available options for our readers in the UK.

THE GRIEF RECOVERY INSTITUTE®

The Grief Recovery Institute has been guided by a primary principle for the past thirty-five years: *to deliver grief recovery assistance to the largest number of people in the shortest period of time.* To meet this goal, the institute initially established Grief Recovery Method Outreach Programs throughout the United States and Canada (now around the world). Feedback from those fledgling groups indicated a clear need for additional support. That led to the first version of *The Grief Recovery Handbook* which John wrote and self-published to meet that demand. The success of the book made it clear that a mainstream publisher might be able to extend our reach and help even more grievers. That led to our long-term collaboration with HarperCollins, which has helped *The Grief Re-*

covery Handbook become available in every community, large and small. With availability of the book has come recovery for upward of one million people so far.

WHY WE WROTE THIS BOOK

As many grievers as we have helped deal with death, divorce, and other losses, there is one major group of people we haven't helped as much as we would like. They are grieving pet owners. This is not to say we haven't tried. We've spent countless hours on the phone with individuals, but they do not usually attend our Grief Recovery Method groups, or see our Grief Recovery Specialists one-on-one. When we encourage them to attend our programs, there's often some trepidation: "You mean I will have to participate alongside people who are working on the death of people?" Many are not willing to attend under those circumstances. They tell us they're afraid they will be judged and dismissed because they are grieving a pet.

This book allows you to take the actions of the Grief Recovery Method without fear of judgment from others. Grief Recovery Method Pet Loss groups, using this book, will be facilitated by our trained specialists. Those groups will focus on pet loss in order to create safety for all.

A PERSONAL NOTE TO YOU, THE READER

We know that if you're reading this book, your heart has been broken by the loss of one or more pets. We know you're looking for effective guidance to help you deal with the emotional changes those losses have made to your life. We know this book can and will help you if you take the actions in it, exactly as outlined. Please don't try to mix and match this book with other ideas. We will be with you every step of the way.

Note*:* As you read the book, you may decide that you need additional help. Look for these trademarks and copyrights to guarantee that you are contacting someone we've trained, who has access to us for guidance in any situation that may need our help. Only we and our Certified Grief Recovery Specialists® are authorized to display these marks:

The Grief Recovery Institute®
The Grief Recovery Method®
Grief Recovery Specialist®
AARAM Formula®
Grief Recovery®

At the end of the book you'll find phone, e-mail, and postal contact information for us.

Visit our website at www.griefrecoverymethod.com to find a Grief Recovery Specialist® in your community.

From our hearts to yours,

Russell, John, and Cole

1

DON'T FEEL BAD,
IT WAS ONLY A . . .

One of the most hurtful comments a grieving pet owner ever hears is, "Don't feel bad, it was only a dog" (or a cat, or a horse, or a parakeet, or a turtle). The statement is thoroughly confusing since it starts by telling you not to feel bad, even though feeling bad or sad is the normal and natural emotional reaction to the death of a pet. It also implies that there is something wrong with you for feeling that way.

Worse, it goes on to minimize the loving relationship you had with your pet by using the word "only," which lands like a dagger in your heart. It's no wonder grieving pet owners are terrified to tell the truth about their feelings. It's also no wonder that they soon begin isolating from people, fearful of hearing more unhelpful comments.

Another comment, almost equally painful is, "Don't feel bad, you can get another dog." It begins with the illogical guidance not to feel bad, even though your heart does. It further minimizes your normal healthy grieving reaction by telling you to just go out and get another dog—as if your relationship with your pet was as replaceable as a broken light bulb and had no emotional strings attached.

Imagine if after your mother died, someone said to you, "Don't feel bad, she was just a woman." Or, "Don't feel bad, just go out and get another mother." Those remarks sound absurd and even cruel.

Compounding the problem is the fact that those comments—and many others—are often delivered by well-intentioned friends or family members. Even though the intent is loving, the impact is not.

AWKWARD GIFT OF A PUPPY OR KITTY

As bad as those hurtful comments can be, we've heard of thousands of incidents where well-meaning people have actually bought a brand-new pet and presented it to grieving people who just experienced a loss. What a difficult gift to receive! A tragic by-product of this kind of unsolicited gift is the large number of dogs and cats who wind up in shelters—and get euthanized.

We hope no one around you has said or done anything that felt bad to you in relation to the death of your pet. But we know that's not likely. While you may be legitimately upset about things people have said to you since your pet died, the fact is that we were all socialized in the same world that gave us so much misinformation about dealing with loss. Our families and friends learned the same unhelpful ideas we did. The probability is that at some time you've made similar incorrect statements to grieving people, whether they were dealing with the death of a pet, a person, or any other significant loss.

YOUR HEART IS BROKEN—NOT YOUR HEAD

The unhelpful comments you've probably heard fall into one of two categories. The first is that they appeal to your intellect, which isn't damaged or broken. We've talked to thousands of grieving people, and we've yet to meet one who called us because their intellect was broken. The second is that they give advice that is difficult or dangerous to follow. For example: being told not to feel bad when your heart is broken.

When people call us, we are often the first to acknowledge the emotional truth about their broken heart. We are total strangers to them, but they have called us because those around them dismissed their emotions with intellectual ideas like, "Don't feel bad, he's in a better place." While an animal that had struggled with a dread disease and then died may be in a better place, we know that the grieving owner is not in a better place. So the probable intellectual truth that the death signals the end of suffering for the pet does not mean an end of emotional suffering for the owner. It actually signals the beginning of emotional pain, not the end. This is just one example where grieving people are given intellectual ideas to try to deal with their emotions.

Grieving people constantly receive advice and it's usually unsolicited and unhelpful. It's right there in, "Don't feel bad, he's in a better place." Look at the first part—don't feel bad. It is advice, even though it makes no sense at all. It is an impossible instruction to follow. How do you *not feel bad* when you feel bad? The unfortunate answer to this question is that most people try to push their emotions down. Worse, after a while, they begin to lie and say they're fine when they're really not. But the advice not to feel bad is rarely singular. "Don't feel bad, you should go right out and get another pet" mixes two pieces of dangerous and incorrect advice into one sentence. We will talk about the second part of this statement under the myth of Replace the Loss in the next chapter.

SELF-IMPOSED SEPARATION ADDS ISOLATION TO SADNESS

Grieving pet owners tend to feel terribly misunderstood. They separate themselves from others out of fear of being judged. That is often the by-product of being subjected to many well-intended but unhelpful comments. The self-imposed separation adds isolation to their sadness. This often causes them to shy away from the very family and friends who should be a source of comfort. Many of our family and friends think what they say will soothe us, but it often makes us seethe. Since we recognize that they mean well, we usually let these comments pass and push our own feelings away.

As this book unfolds, we'll talk about some of the other incorrect comments you may have heard that have contributed to you feeling misunderstood. Some of those unhelpful comments are so common that they have assumed credibility, as if they were true. We'll use some of our own real-life stories to demonstrate the unhelpful information most of us were socialized to believe. After we clear away these unsupportive ideas, you'll be able to take the actions of the Grief Recovery Method outlined in this book.

CONFUSION ABOUT STAGES

Many people are familiar with the pioneering work of Dr. Elisabeth Kübler-Ross, who identified five emotional stages that a *dying* person may go through after being diagnosed with a terminal illness. She identified those stages as denial, anger, bargaining, depression, and acceptance. Unfortunately, over the years, Dr. Ross's work has been shifted from its original focus on the dying process, and misapplied to the grief we feel after someone important to us dies, whether human or animal.

In all our years working with grieving pet owners, we have yet to be approached by someone who was in "denial" that their pet had died. The very first thing they say to us is, "My dog died," or "My cat died," or my horse or other cherished companion.

Those statements reflect absolutely no denial that a loss has occurred. If you are reading this book, *you are not in denial* that you have experienced the death of your pet.

There are no stages of grief. But people will always try to fit themselves into a defined category if one is offered to them. Sadly, this is particularly true if the offer comes from a powerful authority such as a therapist, clergyperson, or doctor.

Do not allow anyone to create any time frames or stages for you.

COMMON RESPONSES

While there are no stages of grief, many grievers do experience some very common responses to loss:

- *Reduced concentration.* A grieving pet owner is in the bedroom. He has an idea about getting something from the kitchen. Upon arrival in the kitchen, he has no earthly idea why he is there or what he went there to get. A preoccupation with the emotions of the loss and an inability to concentrate are nearly universal responses to grief, and can last for weeks, months, or more.

- *A sense of numbness.* Grievers typically report to us that the first reaction they experience after awareness or notification of the death of their pet is a sense of numbness. This numbness can be physical, emotional, or both. The numbness lasts a different length of time for each person. This reaction is often mislabeled as denial.

- *Disrupted sleep patterns.* Grievers report either not being able to sleep or sleeping too much—or both, alternately.

- *Changed eating habits.* Grievers tell us that they have no appetite or that they eat nonstop—or both, alternately.

- *Roller coaster of emotional energy.* Grievers talk about going up and down and in and out of feelings. As a direct result of these emotional highs and lows, grievers often feel emotionally and physically drained.

These are all normal and natural responses to the death of a pet and their duration is unique to every individual. We will not predict for you how long they should last. They do not always occur. They are not stages.

IS RECOVERY FROM GRIEF ACTUALLY POSSIBLE?

Because there's so much misinformation about dealing with loss, most people don't realize that recovery from grief is actually possible. They think the pain of the loss will always be with them. They believe they just have to tolerate the pain and learn to live with it. Or they believe that time will eventually heal their broken hearts if they just wait long enough. Neither of those ideas are accurate, but believing them to be true stops grieving people from looking for solutions.

Fortunately, recovery from grief is possible. You will be able to become emotionally complete with your pet that died. You will be able to have fond memories of that relationship not turn painful. You will be able to remember your pet the way you knew him in life, not just as you remember him in death. Completion of the unfinished emotions attached to this relationship will enable you to be open to another pet at some point in the future. You'll be able to have a unique relationship with a new pet. You'll be able to allow the new pet to have his or her own individual personality, and not be compared to the one that died.

One of the reasons we may think recovery isn't possible is the fact that we don't forget the animals that have been important to us. There's additional confusion because when we remember pets that have been so important to us, we may have feelings of sadness. Many people think that their sadness indicates that something's wrong with them. But sadness is a normal feeling in response to memories about pets that are no longer here. There is a difference between sadness and pain. The Grief Recovery Method will help you deal with the pain caused by the death of your pet. It will allow you to remember and have the normal feelings of sadness and joy when you miss your pet.

GRIEF IS THE NORMAL AND NATURAL REACTION TO LOSS

Many people struggle to understand what grief is. This is due—in part—to the multitude of incorrect ideas they hear as far back as they can remember. The most simple and accurate definition of grief is that it is the *normal and natural reaction to loss*. The range of normal emotions attached to grief is dictated by your unique and individual personality and how you express your feelings. Your grief is about the one-of-a-kind relationship you had with your pet that died. No other person had the same relationship you had with your pet.

Grief is also defined as *the conflicting feelings caused by the end of or change in a familiar pattern of behavior*. When your pet dies, everything familiar for you changes, and with that comes a wide range of emotions as your heart and brain struggle to accommodate the overwhelming feelings of loss. The idea that there are conflicting feelings is best explained when there's been a long-term illness, during which your pet was in a great deal of pain and subjected to all kinds of treatment in an attempt to help. When that pet dies, one of your feelings is likely to be relief that he is no longer in pain. On the other hand, you have tremendous feelings of sadness that a cure did not happen.

We can also say that the intensity of emotion you feel in response to the death of your pet is unique and individual to you and to the one-of-a-kind relationship you had with that pet. No other person can ever feel exactly the same as you feel, even someone else grieving the same pet.

PARTICIPATING IN YOUR OWN RECOVERY

Recovery from loss is the result of a series of small and correct choices. Those choices take the form of actions, which we will outline in this book. Grieving people rarely lack courage or willingness; what they're missing is the correct actions and a safe and loving environment in which to take them. We are going to show you these actions and guide you in taking them. They are actions we've taken to help ourselves and taught to thousands of people just like you.

When people learn that recovery can happen, they are confused about when they could or should start to recover. Because they've been taught that "Time heals all wounds," they think they have to wait a certain time period before they start to recover.

The idea that time can heal is dangerously wrong and we'll discuss this in detail in the next chapter. But for now, here's an example: Imagine that you have seven thorns in your foot. When would you begin to pull them out? Would you wait even a moment before removing them? Would you continue trying to walk while the thorns are still in your foot? Oh, and one more silly question. How many of the thorns would you pull out? The answers to those four questions are painfully obvious, yet many people walk around with emotional thorns in their hearts because they don't know that they can be removed. The essential purpose of this book is to show you how to remove those thorns.

THERE'S NOTHING WRONG WITH YOU

Major losses, including the death of a pet, are not everyday occurrences. When they do occur, it is inevitable that we fall back on whatever information we have learned in the past. Throughout this book, there will be references to the fact that we were socialized incorrectly on the topic of grief. There is also a section in which Cole talks about having been raised with only the best ideas relative to grief and recovery, only to have those ideas trumped by the incorrect ideas prevalent in music, books, TV, and of course, peer pressure.

Most of the initial information—or misinformation—we learn about dealing with grief comes from our family and the immediate society around us. However, nothing that we say here is intended in any way to be a condemnation of anyone's parents, or of society or any institutions. We do not believe that one generation intentionally hands down misinformation to the next. We believe that people teach what they know, because it is most likely what they were taught.

If you have found that the available information and support has not been adequate in helping you deal with the death of your pet, it's not because of what's wrong with you—it's because there is a lack of correct information. If you're reading this book, it means you're open to your grief. It means you're open to beginning a process of recovery, which will enhance your life rather than limit it. If you're reading this book, it's because of what's right with you, not what's wrong.

2

FOUR MAJOR MYTHS
THAT LIMIT US, AND MORE

In our other books and articles, we focus on six myths that limit and restrict us from trusting our normal and natural reactions to loss. But we realize that two of the six aren't always relevant to pet loss. Therefore, we're going to spend more time explaining the four main ones and only briefly touch on the other two.

In the first chapter we used the phrase, "Don't feel bad" nine times. This may give you a hint as to which myth comes first. It may be the most damaging and illogical piece of information we ever learn. But before we launch into this, let us list the four myths we're going to look at in some detail:

- Don't Feel Bad
- Replace the Loss
- Grieve Alone
- Time Heals All Wounds (or, Grief Just Takes Time)

The other two are Be Strong and/or Be Strong for Others, and Keep Busy.

MYTH #1: DON'T FEEL BAD

Children at birth are emotionally honest and stay that way until they are taught to lie about how they feel. By the time children are four or five years old, they've learned that they're not supposed to feel bad or sad, even when bad or sad things happen. In a variety of situations, they hear, "Don't feel bad, here have a cookie," which undermines their natural ability to be emotionally honest. They get this message from their parents, grandparents, teachers, the media, and many other sources.

Our parents' words and ideas are very influential when we're young and have incalculable impact on us, which tends to last indefinitely. The good news is that as you read this chapter, you'll be able to review some of the ideas you learned and have come to believe. You will be able to determine for yourself if they are correct and helpful for you now. If they are not, you'll be able to modify or discard them and become able to deal more effectively with your feelings of loss due to the death of your pet.

THOUSANDS OF REPETITIONS OF "DON'T FEEL BAD" AND "GRIEVE ALONE" BY AGE FIFTEEN

If you think the occasional incorrect emotional guidance by parents about a child's feelings is awkward enough, here's something that will show you the real dimension of the problem. Thirty years ago, a study was released that established that by the time children in our society are fifteen years old, they've already received thousands of messages suggesting that they shouldn't feel bad or sad. And if they do, they should keep it to themselves and not tell—or show—anyone. With that as a backdrop, it's no wonder so many people struggle with their own normal reactions to the death of their pets.

We'll go into more detail later in this chapter about how we learned that we shouldn't talk about our sad or painful feelings. It will be under the myth Grieve Alone.

WE LEARN TO LIE BECAUSE EMOTIONAL TRUTH IS NOT ENCOURAGED OR SUPPORTED

We think you'll agree that feeling bad is the normal and natural reaction to any loss event. Yet the phrase "Don't Feel Bad" is the preamble to many ideas that are aimed at the intellect or give incorrect information. Here's a short list:

- Don't Feel Bad, he's in a better place.
- Don't Feel Bad, at least he didn't suffer.
- Don't Feel Bad, you can get another pet.
- Don't Feel Bad, it was meant to be.
- Don't Feel Bad, God won't give you more than you can handle.

There are more examples, many of which you may have heard, but the bottom line is that you do feel bad when your pet dies. Being told not to feel bad puts you in conflict with your nature. Remember, we talked about how emotionally honest infants and young children are. Since we were subjected to the false idea that we shouldn't feel bad and shouldn't tell others, we learn to keep our feelings inside. When we use our bodies as storage tanks rather than processing plants for the feelings we generate, nothing good can happen.

MYTH #2: REPLACE THE LOSS

For many children, the first major loss that affects their lives is the death of a pet. Often it is a goldfish or a hamster, or it may be a dog or cat, a horse, or a bird. Regardless of the type of animal, the child almost always hears Myth #1, "Don't Feel Bad," followed by, "On Saturday we'll get you a new . . ." We call this "Replace the Loss." It carries implications far beyond the fact that it doesn't make sense to not feel bad when someone you love dies; it also doesn't make sense to rush out and get a new pet when you've barely begun to grieve the death of your pet that just died.

Some of the ongoing effects of replacing the loss come up when we're a little older and we've had our first romantic breakup. That's when we're told, "Don't feel bad, there are plenty of fish in the sea." Again our parents, and others who love us, counsel us not to feel the way we feel and just go out and get a new boyfriend or girlfriend. It doesn't make sense with our pets or in our romantic relationships, but these teachings get passed from one generation to the next. We hope to stem that tide and give better and more helpful guidance for you and for your children.

John's personal story, which is told in the *The Grief Recovery Handbook*, gives a clear-cut example of the first two myths, Don't Feel Bad and Replace the Loss, and how they can affect us all:

When I was born, my family had a dog named Peggy. She adopted me from the moment I arrived home from the hospital. As I grew older, I tried to teach her to retrieve, but she was a Boxer and not really into playing fetch. Peggy always found a way to sleep with me each night. This drove my mother to distraction. But we were persistent and eventually Mom gave up. Then, one morning, I called to Peggy and she wouldn't get up. I remember how cold she felt when I touched her. I remember being afraid. I called to my mother to help me. My mother told me that my dog had died. I'm certain she tried to explain what death was. I'm also certain she didn't know how.

For the next several days after Peggy died, I cried a lot and spent a great deal of time in my room. I'm sure my parents felt inadequate in knowing what to do to help me. Finally, in total

frustration, my dad said: "Don't feel bad—on Saturday we'll
get you a new dog."

    As a young child who wanted his father's approval, this
was a powerful communication from the most important author-
ity figure in my life. I believed my dad and I began to form a
belief about dealing with loss. I tried to follow my father's advice
and not feel bad. I thought that if this is the way he deals with
death, then this is the way I'm supposed to deal with it.

    Sure enough, on Saturday my dad took me to get a new
dog. I still missed Peggy, but I didn't tell my dad or anyone
else. I didn't think they'd approve. After a long period of time I
actually forgot about Peggy. But I also found it hard to love the
new dog in the same way I'd loved Peggy, and I didn't know
why. It's possible, in fact likely, that I couldn't love the new
dog because I wasn't emotionally complete with Peggy.

Peggy's death had a profound emotional impact on John.
That impact was compounded by the powerful and incorrect messages he got from his family—that he shouldn't feel bad, and that
the best way to deal with the pain was to simply replace the loss
and go out and get another dog. That guidance didn't work for
John, but having no better information, he used and reused those
ideas for many years.

    John's story illustrates how much our normal and natural
reaction to loss can be affected by a singular event, especially
when that event happens when we are young. It can set up a
lifetime of incorrect beliefs about dealing with loss. The reason
the incorrect information has such long-lasting effect is because
it usually comes from our parents and other high authority or
influence sources in our lives.

    It was another powerful grief event—the death of his three-
day-old son in 1977—that forced John to realize that trying not to

feel bad in reaction to an emotionally painful event, and replacing the loss, made no sense at all.

NEVER COMPARE AND MINIMIZE

The fact that we mentioned the death of John's son does not mean we are comparing that loss to any other loss. We are not comparing the death of a pet to death of a child, nor to any other loss. All loss is experienced at 100 percent. That doesn't mean that we have the same reactions to all losses, it means that our emotional reaction to the death of our pet (or any other loss) is based on our unique relationship with that individual pet.

It's very important to understand the idea of not comparing losses. In any household, when a pet dies, each member of the family has their own reaction to the death. This is based on their individual and unique relationship with that pet. Since each of us is unique, and since no two relationships are ever the same, no two people will ever have the exact same emotional response to the death of a pet.

We must honor the dignity of our individual grief reactions to the deaths of our pets by never comparing losses and never comparing our emotional responses to those of others.

MYTH #3: GRIEVE ALONE

Grieving people tend to isolate. That's not a natural thing to do—it's something we learn. Remember the study that showed that by the time we're fifteen, we've had thousands of messages suggesting not only that we shouldn't feel bad, but also that we shouldn't tell others those feelings. That constant bombardment to not feel the way we feel or tell others when we have sad or painful feelings leaves us confused about our own nature. It causes us to question ourselves and to isolate from others for fear they will judge us.

What is natural is to share your sad feelings and your happy ones. Think of infants who communicate either their sadness or joy at the top of their lungs. They do this until we start telling them, "Don't feel bad, here have a cookie; you'll feel better." The idea of not feeling bad is compounded by a host of other ideas indicating that we need to hide and isolate our sad feelings from others.

Russell, like John, struggled in similar situations when he had pets die. He tried to talk to his mother about his sad feelings a few weeks after the family's puppy died. His mom said, "Laugh and the whole world laughs with you, cry and you cry alone." Russell knew that his mother wouldn't have intentionally misguided him, but her awareness about grief was limited. She could only pass on what she knew. Because of the importance of his mother in his life, Russell believed her and tried to keep his sadness to himself.

About the same time, he remembers hearing, "Don't burden others with your feelings," as if he had the power to make them feel sad just because he was feeling that way. Sometimes when he was teary at the dinner table, his dad said, "If you're going to cry, go to your room."

Russell had been taught, like John, not to feel bad—even when he did—and to replace the loss when the family pet died. He now had a third incorrect idea: that he mustn't show others how he felt when he felt sad. As he looks back, he realizes that he became an expert at hiding his true feelings, which caused some real problems over his lifetime before he arrived at The Grief Recovery Institute.

MYTH #4: TIME HEALS ALL WOUNDS

The concept that "Time Heals" is probably responsible for more heartache than any other single wrong idea in our society. It's one of those falsehoods that have been passed down from generation to generation. The mistaken idea that after enough time passes something will magically change to make us whole again is preposterous.

If you came across a person or an animal with a broken leg, you wouldn't say, "Time will heal that break." Just as broken bones should be properly set to heal and ultimately function again, so must the *emotional heart.* We all know too many people whose hearts remain broken partly because they are waiting for time to heal them. The sad part is that they've come to believe it's true. People wait around for years with the idea that after a long enough period of time they will feel better again. Some of you reading this book already know this isn't true.

Our favorite way of demonstrating that time can't heal is to ask you to imagine that you discover your car has a flat tire. Would you pull up a chair and sit and wait for air to jump back into the tire? We didn't think so. We know you would take an action. You'd find the jack and the spare tire and change the flat or you'd call the Auto Club to come fix it. Either way, an action would have to be taken before you could get the car back on the road.

Now we ask you to imagine that circumstances have conspired to break your heart. If you're reading this book, this event probably is the death of your pet. We know from our own experience and from helping thousands of others, that time can't heal your broken heart any more than time can fix a flat tire. In either situation, action is the key: either to repair the tire or to reclaim your heart.

We know that time does *not* heal emotional wounds. We also know that unattended grief tends to get worse with the passage of time. We imagine that you know people who are still "stuck" in their grief over a pet, or a person, or another loss after many years, and time still hasn't healed their hearts. We believe that if you're reading this book, you want to learn what you can do to dismiss any of those myths that may be limiting you.

To recap, the four major myths we've just covered are

- Don't Feel Bad
- Replace the Loss
- Grieve Alone
- Time Heals All Wounds

BE STRONG AND KEEP BUSY

There are two other myths we spend a great deal of time on in our other books, but these are less relevant when dealing with the death of a pet. They are Be Strong and Be Strong for Others, and Keep Busy. We want to mention them here because if you were exposed to them in your home or culture, they may limit you in your reaction to the death of your pet.

In simplest terms, we suggest that the idea of "being strong" in the face of sad or painful events is another way we were taught that we shouldn't feel bad and that we shouldn't tell others how we feel. Acting "strong" when we're really sad also gives the wrong verbal and nonverbal communication to other people. It's very confusing when our words and actions don't match our emotions. Many of us learned to say, "I'm fine," when that wasn't true.

As John indicated in his story, this may be because we want the approval of others. In other cases, many of us do it out of a kind of self-defense, because every time we tell the truth about our sad feelings, we're told not to feel that way—that we need to be strong. Also, if we have children, we're told we have to be strong for them.

Being Strong Sends the Wrong Message

John recalls:

When my dog Peggy died, I assumed that my parents were sad too. I think their body language, though not their words, told me so. On several occasions I saw that my mom and dad were sad that Peggy wasn't at the door when they came home. Yet when I asked either of them if they were sad, they said, "No, I'm fine." I remember being confused. As I look back on it now, I realize that they were attempting to "be strong" for me and my brothers. So, what did I learn? I learned that what adults said did not always match what I saw them do when it pertained to sad events.

They told me that death was part of life. Even so, something in me wondered why it wasn't all right to feel sad when something sad happened. Not knowing what else to do, I began to say I was fine even though I was hurting. This pattern was to develop and become an ingrained habit.

Eventually I became so good at hiding my feelings of sadness about everything that I didn't even know I was doing it. At first I learned to hide sad and painful feelings. At nine years of age, I can remember saying to myself, "I'm not going to cry anymore because when you do, people know they've hurt you." I'm sure that at nine years old I had no real idea of how powerfully that message would embed itself in my unconscious mind. Over time I forgot that promise but my unconscious didn't. I

also began to limit happy and joyous feelings as well. For many
years I kept a very tight lid on all of my feelings.

Our last word on the topic of Be Strong is to give you a choice.
You can be strong or you can be human, pick one! We hope you'll go for
human, which is more honest and represents your heart.

Finally, there's Keep Busy. This bad advice is given to grievers all the time. "Keeping Busy" really only acts as a distraction and is based on the false premise that time heals emotional
wounds. The incorrect idea behind keeping busy is that as you
busy yourself doing things, time will pass, and magically, you'll
feel better. This just isn't true.

IDENTIFYING YOUR MYTHS—ACTION #1

We've talked about the fact that grieving people have been taught
to isolate themselves. Your own experience probably confirms
that reality. Since isolation is one of the problems confronting
grieving pet owners, then participation is clearly part of the solu-
tion. In order to encourage you to participate in your own recovery, we're going to suggest that you start right now.

Go back and reread this chapter. Think back on some of the
loss events that have happened in your life, especially when you
were young and still lived with your parents. Think about the
things you heard when your pets or family pets died. Think about
the things you heard or observed in others when a family member
or friend died. Think about the ideas that were said when a relative or family friend had a divorce or romantic ending or when
you had your first breakup.

As you look back, you'll start to realize that a great deal of
what you learned falls under the headings of the myths we've

talked about. You'll also begin to recognize that they probably didn't—and still don't—really help you. Armed with some new ideas about these beliefs, you can consider discarding them. That will allow you to continue reading and taking the actions in this book, which will help you discover and complete what has been left emotionally unfinished by the death of your pet.

Using the list of myths as a guide, think about whether or not you were influenced to believe any or all of them. Take a piece of paper and write down the ones that most affected you and may have limited you. Or you can use the space provided below. In addition to the myths we've listed, see if you can think of any other ideas you were taught or influenced to believe about dealing with sad, painful, or negative feelings that you now realize weren't helpful. Write them down also.

To remind you, here's our list of myths:

- Don't Feel Bad
- Replace the Loss
- Grieve Alone
- Time Heals All Wounds
- Be Strong—Be Strong for Others
- Keep Busy

Notes

_____

_____

_____

_____

_____

SOCIETY OFTEN TRUMPS FAMILY MESSAGES

Cole explains:

Although I grew up with access to the best information possible regarding grief and grief recovery, I too became a victim of what society teaches.

In my home I was never told, "If you're going to cry, go to your room" or "Cowboy up." I saw my dad cry several times with no apologies for his feelings, nor any indication that we weren't allowed to cry as men.

Even though I had gotten the message in my home that it was okay to have feelings and talk about them and even cry, I was still influenced by music, books, TV, and of course my peers, to hide my sad, painful, or negative emotions.

By the time I was a teenager I was clear that as a man you just don't cry. You had to be strong. Period.

The influence of society was powerful and it overrode my family's lessons. I practiced hiding my feelings and became very good at covering up any sad or painful emotions. Looking back, I realize that as many of these pieces of misinformation became linked together, I got good at being strong and if I thought that there was a chance that I was going to cry, I had to isolate so no one would see me cry.

Like so many people, later in life I had to take a hard look at what I had come to believe. Fortunately for me, since my original default information about grief and recovery was correct, it was relatively easy for me to go back to it.

TIME TO DISCARD THE MYTHS

As Cole learned, none of the six myths we've outlined are helpful for anyone in dealing with their broken hearts after their pets have died. Here's one more example of an idea that can limit your ability to deal with the death of your pet.

YOUR VERBAL AND NONVERBAL COMMUNICATION MUST MATCH

Recently, one of our friends said, "It's easier to deal with the death of a pet when you have other pets."

We had a reaction to that comment, which wasn't entirely positive. It's understandable that when you have more than one pet, they still require your care and attention even though one of your other pets has died. Your grief doesn't eliminate their needs for food and attention. But the activities you have to do to care for them, and the love you may give and receive from them, don't diminish the pain or loss you feel about the pet that died. In fact, it's unlikely that you can be with your living pets without being reminded of the one that died.

In this book, we have avoided comparison of pet loss to human loss as much as we could. We want to deviate from that for just a moment and ask this question. If you have three children and one of them dies, does having the other two children make the death of the third easier? We know it's an awkward question, and we know the answer is no. But since our relationships with our pets are individual and unique, as are those with our children, we ask the same question in relationship to your pets. We use the question to illustrate that doubling up your affection for your other pets when one of your pets dies, doesn't effectively help you deal with your grief. You must grieve and complete the unique relationship you had with the pet that died.

We are not animal psychologists and we really can't speak to the nature of the emotions that animals may feel when a member of their extended family dies. However, we do have a sense that most mammals do grieve in some way. We also know that it's unlikely that you can be with your living pets without being reminded of the one that died.

The animals that are attached to us pick up cues from our body language and from our tone of voice when we talk. With those things in mind, we believe that your communication relative to your grief must be honest. If you try to "be strong" or hide your feelings, you will mislead your pets, because what you say and the body language you demonstrate will not match up to what you are actually feeling. We suggest that you talk openly and honestly to your living pets about the feelings of sadness you have about your pet that died. Your emotional truth can't hurt them, but covering up your real feelings can be very confusing.

In concluding this chapter, we hope you'll be willing and even eager to discard the myths that have limited you and may have made you feel there was something wrong with you in your reaction to the death of your pet. As we said at the end of the first chapter—if you're reading this book, it's because of what's right with you, not what's wrong.

3

SHORT-TERM ENERGY RELIEVING BEHAVIORS (STERBS)

The death of our pets naturally produces an incredible amount of emotional energy, but since we've all been socialized from early on to deal with sad, painful, and negative emotions incorrectly, we tend to store the energy inside ourselves. Making it worse, we learn very quickly that many of our friends and family don't understand the level of emotion we experience when our pet dies, as suggested by the title of our first chapter, "Don't Feel Bad, It Was Only a . . ."

Confronted with that comment, we're even more likely to push our feelings down and not share how we feel with anyone. We can't tell you how many grieving pet owners have called us with the complaint that even their spouse didn't understand the emotions they were having when their pet died.

The most clichéd of stories illustrates how early in our lives we're encouraged to move away from our natural emotional reactions to any kind of loss. A little child has come home from preschool with her feelings hurt by events with the other children on the playground. Mom, Dad, Grandma, or any other caretaker says, "What happened?" The child responds, tearfully, that one of the kids has been mean to her. The caretaker says, "Don't cry, here have a cookie; you'll feel better," thus setting the child up with a lifetime belief, from an important authority source, that *feelings can be fixed with food.*

Let's look at food more closely now. Upon eating the cookie, the child feels *different*, not better, and for the moment is distracted and forgets about the incident on the playground. However, there has been no completion of the emotional pain caused by the event. The event and the feelings attached to it are now buried under the cookie, the sugar, and the distraction. If the child were to bring it up sometime later, she would probably be told, "We don't cry over spilled milk," as if to say that it's not okay to bring it up again. So it must stay buried.

Since we learn to cover up, hide, or bury our feelings under food when we are very young, it's not surprising that sometime later some of us adapt that same behavior and start covering up our feelings under alcohol or other drugs. Observing family members at funerals or wakes consuming large amounts of food and alcohol may have reinforced that idea. Consuming food or alcohol in response to the emotional energy created by the death of our pet doesn't help us discover or complete the source of the energy or complete the relationship with the pet. Therefore, we are participating in an *illusion* that the short-term relief offered by food or alcohol gives us any long-term relief from the pain caused by the death.

Food and alcohol are obvious and typical short-term energy relieving behaviors. There are many, many other short-term behaviors that have the same life-limiting and damaging consequences. Here is a partial list of other behaviors that, if done for the *wrong reasons*, can have a negative impact on grieving people:

- Anger
- Exercise
- Fantasy (movies, TV, books, Internet, texting, video games)
- Isolating
- Sex

- Shopping (humorously called "retail therapy")
- Workaholism

Most of these actions are not harmful in and of themselves. They become harmful when you engage in them for the wrong reasons. Just as eating a cookie does not help the emotional pain, shopping provides no long-term help for the pain caused by the death of your pet. In fact, it can have quite the opposite effect. The shopping binge is often followed by remorse over the wasted money. This is a further distraction from the real and original emotional event—the death of your cherished companion.

At the end of this chapter, after we've explained a little more about STERBs, you will have an opportunity to look at your own actions from the perspective of dealing indirectly with the feelings caused by your loss.

SHORT-TERM RELIEF DOESN'T WORK

Imagine a steam kettle. The kettle is filled with water. The flame under the kettle is turned up high. Normally, as the water heats and boils, the steam generated by the heat is released through the spout. Most kettles are fitted with a whistle to notify us when they have reached the boiling point. Imagine that same steam kettle filled with water, with a high flame burning below, but now there is a cork jammed into the spout. Imagine the pressure that builds up inside that kettle when the spout cannot release the built up energy. The cork represents a lifetime of misinformation that causes us to believe that we are not supposed to talk about sad, painful, or negative emotions.

A functioning steam kettle releases energy immediately as it builds up. When you're told, "Don't feel bad," and "If you're going to cry, go to your room," the energy stays inside you. The major myth that "Time will heal" is laughable if you think of the steam kettle analogy. Time will only move the steam kettle closer to an explosion.

As the pressure builds up inside our personal steam kettle, we automatically seek relief. This is when we may start participating in short-term energy relieving behaviors (STERBs). There are three major problems with STERBs. The first is that they work, or more accurately, they *appear* to work. They create an illusion of recovery by causing you to forget or bury emotions. The second problem with STERBs is that they are *short-term*. They do not last, and they do not deal with the true emotional issue. And lastly, they do nothing to remove the cork that is jammed in the spout. In fact, most people don't even realize that there *is* a cork in the spout.

Eventually our steam kettle is overloaded and the STERBs no longer create the illusion of well-being. Imagine what might happen if a major loss event, like the death of a pet, is added to an internal collection of unresolved emotions. It might put such a strain on our corked kettle as to actually cause an explosion.

While some emotional explosions are huge and make national headlines, most are much smaller. Here is an unfair question. Have you ever had an emotional explosion larger than circumstances called for? Sadly, we know that you all have to say yes. Over time, we develop the habit of putting a cork in our own personal steam kettles. We bottle up our own feelings, because we have been taught to do so.

Taking the actions in this book will help you remove the cork. You will then be able to deal more effectively with the emotions associated with the death of your pet. In order to remove the cork, we've been looking at the ideas that created the cork. They are represented by the myths we discussed in the last chapter. You're getting ready to discard and then replace those myths with more accurate ideas about dealing with sad emotions. You're also learning that STERBs are not really helpful. As you recognize this, you'll be able to take the correct and helpful actions in this book to help you deal with the emotions caused by the death of your pet.

A simple analogy: if your yard is full of weeds, you can cut the weeds to give some short-term relief (but they will grow back), or you can pull the weeds and eliminate the problem. You are arriving at the point of making a decision: short-term or long-term relief? We want you to commit to long-term, and we will guide you and help you along the way.

JUMPING FROM STERB TO STERB

When Russell's marriage ended, his wife left California, leaving their Siberian husky, Tasha, with him. He wasn't able to take care of his business and a rambunctious young dog. He had to give her up. Fortunately, he was able to rehome her with a friend who lived near the beach in Malibu. He was heartbroken to part with her, but thrilled at the life she got to lead at the beach.

After Tasha moved away, Russell started having a couple of drinks every night, all by himself. After a few months, that stopped working for him, and he switched to a different STERB. Of course, back then, he didn't know what a STERB was. As he reflects on it now, he realizes that he had a tremendous amount of emotional energy not only about his relationship with Tasha, but about his divorce from Vivienne, and he had no awareness of what to do to deal with his grief in regard to either of those losses.

IDENTIFYING YOUR STERBS—ACTION #2

Your next recovery action is to identify the short-term energy relieving actions you have used or may be using to try to escape the pain caused by the death of your pet. Start by reading this chapter again. Try to identify at least two examples of short-term relief you have used to displace your feelings since this loss happened. This is not as easy as it appears. It could be your first chance to demonstrate your commitment to total honesty.

As you begin this exercise, you might think of STERBs you participated in at other times in your life, following other losses, not just the death of a pet. If that happens, let it be okay with you. Here is the list of short-term energy relieving behaviors from earlier in the chapter. Use it as a guideline to help determine if you have been relying on short-term relief:

- Food
- Alcohol/Drugs
- Anger
- Exercise
- Fantasy (movies, TV, books, Internet, texting, video games)
- Isolating
- Sex
- Shopping (humorously called retail therapy)
- Workaholism

Using a clean sheet of paper, or the lines provided below, copy the short-term energy relievers from our list in which you have participated. Then add any others that you discover. It is actually very common in our society to have been socialized with the idea of covering up emotional pain rather than confronting it directly.

Notes

_____

_____

_____

_____

_____

_____

We conclude this chapter by telling you not to judge yourself if you realize that you've relied a great deal on short-term relief. If you have, it's because you didn't know what else to do. It's important that you be able to recognize your short-term relieving behaviors. Those behaviors may be a tip-off that you are emotionally incomplete with something that's currently happening in your life, or with something from your past that has been reignited.

4

YOUR HISTORY OF PET LOSSES

L osses that occur when we are young influence how we deal with our grief. We observe and record the actions and words of the people around us, especially the adults, who are our tour guides. Some of what the adults do and say about their own grief and ours is correct, but a lot of it isn't. Unfortunately, when we're young, we don't have a way to differentiate between what's right and what's wrong. So we assume that everything the adults do is correct, and we copy it. That's why this next exercise is so important. It will help you see what you know and believe—and whether those ideas are correct and helpful for you as you deal with the impact of the death of your pet.

Most of the animals that are likely to be our domestic companions have relatively short life spans. There's a high probability that you've experienced more than one pet loss. If that's true for you, we'll soon have you make a list of those losses, going back as far as you can recall.

Special Note: For those of you who've only experienced the death of one pet, you can make a list of some of the other losses that have affected you. They could be deaths of people; divorces or other romantic endings; career, health, or faith issues; and other losses. Think back especially to any of those kinds of losses that happened when you were a child. And then think about what you learned or observed in your family about dealing with those losses. Was there open talk about people's grief, or was it hidden? Was it safe for you to talk about your feelings, or not?

Taking a little time to think about those things and making some notes about them will help you understand what ideas—helpful or not—you've brought to the death of your pet.

There are several reasons for this exercise. Primary among them is that as each of your pet losses happened, you were learning what to do—or not do—in reaction to the emotions you felt. And for those of you who just have the one current pet loss, looking back at other losses will help you see what you learned, in general, about dealing with your grief. It's often in the aftermath of those events that we hear the four myths and other misinformation that trap us in our grief and keep us from recovery. Awareness of some of the beliefs you may have developed—even if you didn't realize them before—will help you discard the unhelpful ones and become willing and able to adopt new, more helpful ideas.

We will go first and demonstrate two of our Pet Loss Histories to show you how. We'll begin by creating a Pet Loss History Graph, followed by a brief description of the entries on the graph.

RUSSELL'S PET LOSS HISTORY GRAPH

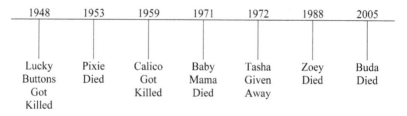

BORN: 1943

1948	1953	1959	1971	1972	1988	2005
Lucky Buttons Got Killed	Pixie Died	Calico Got Killed	Baby Mama Died	Tasha Given Away	Zoey Died	Buda Died

1948—Neighbor's Dog, Lucky Buttons, Got Killed.

When I was five, living in Rochester, New York, my family took our neighbor's dog on an outing in the country. On the way back we had the windows open in the car. Lucky Buttons jumped out and got hit by a car and died. My parents told me not to feel bad—it was an accident, but I did feel bad, and being told not to feel that way confused me.

1953—Our New Puppy, Pixie, Died. We had moved from an apartment building to a house in North Miami, Florida. Now we could have a dog. We got a Jack Russell mix. My sisters and I named her Pixie. At the time, my mother had loaded up our freezer with cuts of meat wrapped in aluminum foil. When she took the meat out of the packages, she'd let the dog lick the foil. The dog got aluminum poisoning and died. My mother felt terrible, of course, and I was really sad. This is when my mother said, "Laugh and the whole world laughs with you; cry and you cry alone." We got a cat shortly after Pixie died, and it definitely came under the heading of replace the loss.

1959—Free-Spirited Calico Got Killed. We had a cat named Calico, whom we got very soon after our dog Pixie died. Although Calico lived and dined with us, he was a nighttime prowler. He'd often come home with cuts and scratches, and even once with a piece of his ear missing. One day we found him dead near the street. He'd been shot. Although I'd never really had much of a relationship with him, I was affected by his death and by how he died. My family didn't talk about it, so I thought I just had to cover up how I felt.

1971—Baby Mama and Thirty Pet Rats. My wife and I had done a favor for a neighbor in our apartment building. We agreed to look after her four pet rats while she went away for a long weekend. The long weekend turned out to be forever. We became the confused owners of three adult rats—two male and one female, and a very young female. We named them Papa, Mama, Uncle, and Baby Rat. Baby Rat became a personal pet. She would lick our feet dry when we came out of the shower. She would sit on our shoulders and groom our hair. Baby Rat didn't stay a baby for long, and she soon became pregnant. We renamed her Baby Mama. Baby Mama got pregnant again and again, and our family got even bigger. At one point we had more than thirty rats, but only Baby Mama ever became a real pet. Eventually she developed an inner ear problem that rats are prone to and started turning around in endless circles. We took her to our chiropractor who actually gave her an adjustment. It worked, but only for a few days. When Baby Mama died, we were grief stricken. We didn't realize what an incredible bond we had with her, and we didn't know how to deal with our emotions.

1972—Tasha, the Siberian Husky. When my wife Vivienne and I divorced, I became the sole guardian of our highly energetic young husky, Tasha. At the time, I owned a restaurant which demanded almost all my waking hours, seven days a week. The little house I rented didn't have a yard, and I wasn't able to get Tasha the kind of exercise she needed. Fortunately, I was able to rehome her with a friend who lived near the beach in Malibu. Although I was heartbroken to part with her, I was thrilled at the life she got to lead living at the beach.

1988—Zoey, the Lab–Great Dane Mix. Zoey was Alice's dog that adopted me when Alice and I became a couple. Zoey got cancer. I'd only known her about a year, but we were very close. One day, about two weeks before she died, we were in the waiting room at the vet's office. An elderly gentleman sitting near us overheard that Zoey didn't have long to live. He said, "When she dies, you should go right out and get another dog." Fortunately, I had learned how to respond. I said, "Thanks, I really appreciate your concern," and I turned back to Alice. In that situation, I was a griever, not an educator. I didn't need to distract myself from the primary emotional issue of Zoey's health by delivering a lecture about *replace the loss*.

2005—Buda Died. The long story of Buda, the Hungarian Vizsla, appears later in this book. The short story is that Buda was my heart and soul. On Friday, he seemed to be the healthiest dog on planet earth. The next day, he seemed a little out of sorts. On Sunday I took him to the vet, where he was diagnosed with terminal, inoperable cancer. He was a rescue, who we thought was only about six and a half years old. The vet that Sunday thought he was closer to ten. No matter his age, the shock and devastation of the diagnosis was chilling. I was scheduled to fly to New York on Monday morning, to be on the *Today Show* with Matt Lauer. We delayed the end until I got back. On Thursday morning we were at the vet's office for the last moments of Buda's life. The next several weeks were among the most emotional of my life. The tears were constant.

COLE'S PET LOSS HISTORY GRAPH

BORN: 1981

8 Years Old	10 Years Old	19 Years Old	20 Years Old	26 Years Old
Lost Ninja	Put Max Down	Gave Away Frankie Four Fingers	Figuero Died	Put Bull Down
				Put Gemini Down

Ninja: Ninja was my first dog. I remember when our family moved from an apartment building to a house and the excitement I felt at getting the news that I could finally have a dog. We went to the pound and I got to pick him out. He was a beautiful shepherd mix. I bonded with him instantly. But as close as we became, he had other plans. He had a strong desire to explore and was constantly escaping from our backyard. We were always tracking him down in the neighborhood after one of his escapes. One day during a rainstorm, he ran away and we never found him. We put up flyers and looked for him for weeks. I felt terrible about it, as if we had let him down. Not knowing what happened to Ninja was very painful for me.

Max: After Ninja ran away, my parents made sure *not* to teach me to *replace the loss*. They encouraged me to talk openly about my feelings and never told me I shouldn't feel the way I did. After some time, I felt ready to begin a relationship with another dog. We went to the pound and I found Max. He was a great-looking black Lab mix and very sweet. He loved to lick my face and I loved having another furry friend. We had him for three years and he slept at the foot of my bed every night. We were best buddies! Whenever I came in the door, Max would rush to greet me and lick my face. One day I came home from school and immediately knew something was not right. Max didn't greet me at the door—he just stood near the fireplace. I went over to greet him and he growled at me. That scared me, as he had never shown me anything but love. I went closer to him and he growled at me again and backed up into the fireplace, singeing his tail, and then he ran into the backyard. I started to cry. I knew something was very wrong. At that point, my mom heard the commotion and came into the living room. I told her what happened. We found an overturned trash basket in our guest room where a friend of the family was staying. Max had gotten into some medication that our guest had thrown out. We called the vet, told him what was happening, and read him the label on the prescription bottle. He told us that there was nothing he could do for Max. He said Max would not make it, and in the meantime it would be excruciatingly painful. We went outside to find Max vomiting blood and trembling. I was terrified, unable to help the animal I loved so much. My mom called my dad and they realized we had to put Max out of his misery. Dad rushed home and used a pistol to end Max's agony. I was inside, looking through the window. I was horrified at what was happening, but I knew that it was the right thing to do so that he didn't suffer any longer.

Frankie Four Fingers: He was a very cool Australian bearded dragon. His main diet was crickets. I always loved taking him out of his terrarium so he could hang out on me. He liked my body heat. Eventually I gave him to my friend's little brother. I felt bad since I had committed to take care of him and didn't keep my word. I always hoped he was cared for properly, and I felt sad that I had given him away.

Figuero: Figuero was a beautiful black cat with stunning green eyes. We called her the princess of the night. She was a tough, scrappy cat, and she was free to roam in and out of the house. From time to time, she would come back with a nick out of her ear or some other injury. She got along great with all of us. She had great confidence and didn't take any nonsense from our dogs. When she was about five years old, we were told that she had cancer and wouldn't live much longer. Tough as she was, she lived another nine years. I got the news that she had died when I was away at college and I was sad that I never got to say good-bye to her.

Bull: Bull was a pit/lab mix with great brindle markings. He loved people but did not like other dogs. The only other dog he liked was our Doberman, Gemini. I will never forget the first day we brought him home. Gemini the older, bigger dog decided to take away Bull's chew bone. The growl that came out of that pup was almost impossible to believe. We were all surprised and laughed at Gemini who got the message loud and clear. She never tried to take his bone again. The sight of that big Doberman backing off from the puppy is a picture I'll never forget.

Bull was very powerful. Everyone in the family felt protected when he was around. He was a loyal friend to me starting when I was in middle school. After I went away to college, I missed him; I was sad that I wasn't around him every day as I was when I lived at home. When I went home on holidays, I saw that his health was starting to decline. We worried about his quality of life. He was retreating more and more into my parents' spare bedroom. When it was time to help Bull die I came home and as a family we said all the things we needed to say to him before the vet gave him the last shot. It was one of the most emotionally painful things I'd ever been through. I was proud that I was there for him at his final moment on this earth, but I was very sad and knew I would miss him terribly. He was a great dog.

Gemini: Gemini—our neurotic, sweet, loving Doberman. I remember the day we picked her up from the breeder. We played with all the pups and finally chose her. In truth, she chose us. She pulled every cute puppy trick and we fell for it. We named her Gemini on the car ride home. She was very scared the first few weeks at our house, away from her mom and littermates. I remember sleeping with her on the kitchen floor to comfort her. Soon she was part of our family. One day when we came home, she made a face that showed her teeth. At first I was scared, remembering what had happened with Max. After a second though, we realized it wasn't aggression—she was grinning at us. She couldn't contain her excitement and broke out in a Doberman version of a smile. It was something I came to love about her. Although Gemini was really my mom's dog, she had been part of my life for a very long time. When it was time for her to go, I remember crying uncontrollably as I said my final good-bye to her. I realize now that some of my emotion was about Bull, who had died before her, and how important those two dogs had been to me all those years in my life at home with my parents.

CREATING YOUR PET LOSS HISTORY GRAPH—ACTION #3

All you need for this exercise is a piece of paper, on which you'll write down a list of your pets that have died. You can put the year or specific date down if you remember it, or the approximate age you were when it happened. Don't be preoccupied if your memory is not exact about those details. It's more important to recall your feelings about the loss and what was said or demonstrated to you about it by your parents or others.

You can follow the example in Russell's list by putting the year and the name of the pet, and then writing a few sentences about one of the most vivid memories that comes to mind. It is also helpful to add something about the ending of the pet's life and the feelings you had when he died. Or you could use Cole's example and just start with the name of the pet and a few memories and the ending.

You may have had some pets when you were very young, like turtles or hamsters, and you don't remember their names. In some cases, like goldfish, you may never have named them. That's okay. More important is what happened when they died. It's not uncommon to have had a goldfish not be there when you got home from school. Your mom or dad may have told you a story, but later you found out they'd flushed it down the toilet. That can be upsetting to a child.

There may have been a little memorial ceremony and a burial in a box in the backyard. There may have been some helpful things said, or some things that you found troubling. This is what you put on the paper. Recall that in Russell's Pet Loss History, he reported that his parents often told him not to feel bad, even though he did. You may also have been told not to feel bad, and promised that you'd get another pet right away. And you probably heard the false idea that time heals emotional wounds. All of that misinformation may have been going into your young mind as if it were true.

What we're told and what we observe when we're young tends to stick with us forever. This is an opportunity to see what you learned and may have been using in dealing with your grief that isn't working for you now.

Reminder, for those of you who have only experienced the death of one pet: You can make a list of some of the other losses that have affected your life. They could be deaths of people; divorces or other romantic endings; or career, health, or faith issues.

Set aside somewhere between 30 and 45 minutes. Have a box of tissues handy: it might be emotional for you as you remember the pets that have been part of your life. But don't be preoccupied if it's not emotional. The only requirement is that you be honest.

When you finish your Pet Loss History Graph, congratulate yourself. It requires courage and willingness, along with correct guidance, to take these actions. You can take a break, call it a day, or read forward to the next actions in the book.

5

PREPARING TO REVIEW
THE RELATIONSHIP

In moving toward being able to become emotionally complete with your pet that has died, we first asked you to look at the fact that you may have learned some incorrect ideas about dealing with grief. We discussed several of the myths that are passed from generation to generation without question or investigation. In addition to the ones we mentioned, you may have recalled others that were unique to your family, your culture, or even your neighborhood. By now, you may realize that many of the ideas you carried forward were not helpful to you in prior losses, and therefore are of limited value as you deal with the painful reality of the death of your pet.

Next, after discussing the myths, we helped you add another new awareness related to the high probability that you've been storing feelings inside your body. Now you know that's not the best idea. If you're ready to stop using your body as a tea kettle with a cork in the spout, then let's set aside all your STERBs for now and activate your courage and willingness and get ready to get to work.

Lastly, as a result of creating a Pet Loss History Graph, you are more aware of what you learned in reaction to the losses you listed; you may have a greater sense of some of the limitations that the myths put on your emotions or the ability to express them. For those of you who've only had one pet loss, you may have realized the same kinds of limitations by looking at some of your other losses.

We'll soon show you how to review your entire relation-ship with your pet, but first we're going to give you some helpful information about the nature of those relationships and about the concept of emotional completion.

YOUR PET NEVER SAID YOU WERE
FAT, UGLY, OR STUPID

Because of the unique connections between our differing species, the relationships we carve out with animals tend to be almost ex-clusively positive. Yes, there are the occasional glitches, and the odd resistances or belligerence with our four-footed, winged, or slithering domestic companions. But in the main, they are posi-tive, mutually satisfying relationships with benefits all around.

Our relationships with our pets do not usually contain the plots and subplots, the machinations and motivations that are part and parcel of our human-to-human bonds. It's unlikely that your pets ever hurt your feelings, or lied to you, or cheated and robbed you (though from time to time they may have been known to steal and hide or destroy your shoes or your prized possessions). But we're sure you know what we mean.

There's a unique, heartwarming devotion—usually in both directions—between humans and pets. For most of us, the thing that charms our hearts is the absolute and unconditional accep-tance of us—by our pets—just the way we are, warts and all.

AN UNINTENTIONAL BENEFIT

For those of us who help grieving pet owners, there has been an unintentional but heart-opening benefit attached to the experiences we've had when our pets died. It has helped us understand the depth of emotion that can happen when the pets we love die. With that awareness, we are able to really "hear" the hearts of the callers who often tell us it feels like they've had more feeling with the death of their pet than when their parent or another person died. Many people might be aghast at that, or not understand it. It may seem to be a comparison, but it really isn't. It's just someone trying to explain how much heartbreak they feel when their pet dies.

A HEART WITH EYES

Our relationships with our pets are unique to each of us and are very emotional. *We'll help you honor your relationship by looking at it with a particular set of eyes—the eyes that are attached to your heart—to look inward at the incredible loving connection you experienced with your pet.* As we move forward, we'll be asking you to look at the entire relationship, not just the ending, but all of it, from as far back as you can recall.

RELATIONSHIP ASPECTS— PHYSICAL, EMOTIONAL, SPIRITUAL

Relationships can have many aspects, but the three we're most concerned with are the physical, the emotional, and the spiritual. When our pets die, the direct physical relationship has ended. We can no longer touch them or interact with them in the same way. But, to the best of our knowledge, our emotional and spiritual relationships go on after they die—at least as long as we're alive. While that's true, there must be a shift in the emotional and spiritual elements of the relationship. This in turn allows those aspects of the relationship to continue in their most positive form after the death.

The purpose of this book and the actions you're taking is to enable you to complete what was left emotionally unfinished by the death. As a result, you will be able to establish a new emotional and spiritual relationship based on feeling more complete with what did and didn't happen between you and your pet.

The events that occur over the duration of a relationship cause a wide range of emotional reactions for us. Fortunately, with our pets, most of the emotions are positive, with only rare forays into unpleasant events. However, even in the most ideal relationships, there are always things we wish had been "different, better, or more," and there are always unrealized "hopes, dreams, and expectations" about the future. For example, if there had been an illness and some suffering, you will have wished that your pet had not had pain. Or, if there had been an accident, you might replay it in your mind many times, especially as it relates to anything you could have done differently that might have prevented it. And in those instances where your pet displayed bad behavior, you will have wished that it had learned to act better. As you move forward in this book, keep those six words—*different, better, more, hopes, dreams, expectations*—in mind. They will help you discover what may have been left emotionally incomplete.

THE DANGER OF ENSHRINEMENT

Because our relationships with our pets tend to be overwhelmingly positive, grieving pet owners sometimes enshrine those relationships. They focus only on fond memories. Where incomplete grief is concerned, this is known as "enshrinement." Enshrinement, in its most damaging form, can include obsessively building memorials to the pet that died. One of the ways this can be demonstrated is by keeping large numbers of objects that represent the pet, or by constant comparison to any new pet you later acquire.

Less critical but equally limiting can be the enshrinement that simply doesn't allow the griever to look accurately at all aspects of the relationship. Many grievers limit their thoughts and feelings to fond memories or positive comments about their pet that died. But all relationships include both positive and negative interactions. We know that you can complete your grief only by being totally honest about the relationship you had with your pet.

Bedevilment is the opposite of enshrinement, in which a griever tends to have a litany of complaints about a relationship. Bedevilment is very rare among grieving pet owners, but stay alert in case you notice that you are focused on the negatives to the exclusion of the other aspects of the relationship.

GRIEF IS EMOTIONAL

Regardless of age, expected life span, or cause of death, you will have an emotional reaction to the death of your pet. Anything else would not be normal. But one of the more typical reactions is a sense of numbness, especially in the first few days or weeks after the death. It's as if our brain shuts us down like a circuit breaker so we don't feel the enormity of the pain. In a sense, the numbness represents an overwhelming amount of feeling rather than being an indication of no feelings. It's also true that not all of us experience emotions the same way or within the same time frame, so this is another reminder not to compare your feelings—or lack of them—to anyone else's.

Part of the objective in reading this book and taking the actions it suggests is to enable you to retain fond memories and the feelings of love and connection you had with your pet, even though the physical aspect of the relationship has ended. It's usually not enough just to say "I loved him. I miss him." While those statements are emotionally accurate, they don't represent the depth and intensity of a long-term relationship with powerful emotional bonds. Although some relationships with pets are cut very short by illness or accidents, the end of those relationships can still have maximum emotional impact.

WHAT IS COMPLETION?

We've used the words *complete, completion,* and *incomplete* many times up until this point, usually connected to the words *emotional* or *emotionally.* We've also used the phrase *emotionally unfinished* a few times. You may have a sense of what we mean, but if not, we'd like to clarify it now, since in the opening pages we made a promise, which was, "When you take the actions suggested in this book, you will be able to become *emotionally complete* with your pet that died."

Earlier in this chapter we said that even in the most ideal relationships, there are always things we wish had been "different, better, or more," and there are always unrealized "hopes, dreams, and expectations" about the future. With those words in mind, we can now explain a little more about what completion is.

It's one thing to have our memories and the emotions that attach to them. It's another thing to learn to complete the unfinished or undelivered emotions that are part of those memories. This is not always the easiest concept to grasp and accept, because it can be interpreted to mean that there's something wrong with you or the loving relationship you had with your pet. That's not what we mean. What we mean is that the death may have left you feeling emotionally unfinished.

It may be easier to understand what we mean if you think about arguments you've had with the people in your life. When you reflect on those interactions, you can easily realize that there were things that you wish you had said or done differently. This becomes especially meaningful if the other person dies before you have a chance to straighten things out.

Generally we won't have had arguments with our pets, but we're often left feeling unfinished with things we'd hoped to do with them but never did. Russell had always wanted to take his dog to the beach to run, but never got around to it. When Buda died, one of Russell's first thoughts was that he never got to see him running on the beach.

Probably the biggest category of incomplete grief with our pets is the issue of "more." The fact is that you never get enough of someone you love. Even when an animal has lived the full—or even beyond—expected life span, you're left feeling robbed of more time with them.

Part of what makes our relationships with our pets different from our human ones is that there aren't usually as many things that fall into the idea of "different," as it relates to day-to-day interactions. It's when you start thinking about some of the events that surround the end of your pet's life that you might find yourself questioning decisions you had to make. If you think about it, you'll realize that those decisions, which were often about medical concerns, were not directly about your long-term emotional relationship with your pet. But since you felt responsible for your pet's well-being, the end-of-life issues can become very emotional for you as you go over and over the circumstances that led up to the death.

Over the years, we've received thousands of phone calls from grieving pet owners. Most of the calls are focused either on the griever's false sense of guilt, which keeps them trapped, or on the endless telling of a painful story, which keeps them stuck like a hamster on a wheel.

By the time you got this book, you might have told the story of "what happened" at the end of your pet's life many times to friends and family. Yet you may still be having a difficult time adapting to your life, and the changes you perceive, as the result of the absence of your companion. You may have begun to realize that repeating the story is not freeing you from the painful feelings you have concerning whether or not you did the right things. We've known people to get caught in that kind of loop for many years, some even for decades, as they replay the circumstances over and over in their hearts and their heads. Sadly, it does very little of value for those people and tends to isolate them further from the people—and even other animals—who are or might be part of their lives.

Here are those two scenarios, one related to guilt, and the other to the endless retelling of the story.

GUILT IS RARELY THE RIGHT WORD

An often-misused word applied to grief is guilt. We call it the "G" word. We never introduce that word because it is rarely the right word.

Many grieving pet owners call us and tell us that they feel guilty about something that happened near the end of their pet's life. Our response is to ask them if they ever did anything with intent to harm their pet. The almost universal response is "No!"

At that point we explain that the dictionary definition of guilt implies intent to harm. Since they just told us they didn't do anything with intent to harm their pet, we recommend they put the G word back in the dictionary. Then we suggest that they are probably devastated enough by the death of their pet that they don't need to add to it by hurting themselves with an incorrect word that distorts their feelings.

Then we ask them if there are some things they wish had ended differently, better, or more. The almost universal response to that question is "Yes!" And then the floodgates open, and they tell us what they wish had been different, better, or more.

Without the useful guidance to identify different, better, or more, grieving pet owners stay stuck on ideas like guilt and are unable to take responsibility for their reaction to the death of their pet. Without that awareness and responsibility, they are helpless to recover.

WHAT HAPPENED—THE ENDLESS LOOP

When grieving pet owners call us, we usually start the conversation with the question "What happened?" In response, the caller often starts to recite a litany of the events and procedures at the vet's office or clinic during the last days, weeks, or months of their pet's life. While they seem to need to tell those stories, we know they have limited value for them. Worse, we know that even though the wrong diagnosis or wrong meds may be important details, they can keep the griever away from the essential issue, which is their relationship with their pet that died. We sometimes get the sense that the griever has told the story before, often several times, but is caught in an endless loop.

*Our job on those phone calls is to acknowledge that while the details about the death are important, ultimately their grief is about the **fact** that their pet died and their relationship with that pet, not only about how it happened. We then help them tell us a little about the relationship they had with their pet*

*during its lifetime and what he or she meant to them emotion-
ally. From that point we can guide them to the actions as they
appear in this book, which help them jump off that storytelling
loop that never ends. Taking the actions helps them complete
what was emotionally unfinished for them in their relationship
with their pet, as well as in relationship to the events at the end
of the pet's life.*

MORE ABOUT COMPLETION

It's very likely that you've heard things like, "You have to let go,"
"You have to move on," and "Life goes on." We'd be willing to
bet that you've become both tired of and even offended by those
comments. While they are well-intended, they don't really mean
anything of value in terms of your grief. Worse, they do nothing
to help you accomplish the very things they suggest. It's intellec-
tually accurate to suggest that our lives go on after someone else's
life has ended. But that doesn't address the presenting emotional
issues, which have to do with your broken heart. Nor does it address the fact that you miss your pet and may not feel much like
participating in life.

What you're about to do will help you be able to let go of the
pain you may feel and to move forward in your life, even though
things are different than they were before the death of your pet.
It's time for you to take the next important actions of the Grief
Recovery Method that will allow you to achieve the three major
objectives we mentioned in the opening pages of this book:

- To have fond memories of your relationship with your pet
  not turn painful

- To be able to remember your pet the way you knew him in life, not only as in death
- To have a life of meaning and value, even though your life will be different

DON'T STOP YOURSELF

Years ago we wrote an article called "Legacy of Love or Monument to Misery." In it we talked about the fact that so many people live in pain for a very long time following the death of someone meaningful to them. It's as if they believe their pain is equal to the love they had. In the article, we suggested that *pain does not equal love—pain equals pain.* We've heard from many grieving pet owners who also trap themselves in the idea that their pain is an expression of their love.

It's very important to complete the unfinished aspects of any relationship so that we can achieve our real goals of maintaining the loving memories and feelings as long as we are alive. Completing what is unfinished allows us to finally get off the endless-story-pain loop. *Then love can equal love.*

Recovery from grief is not an accident, nor is it a function of time passing. As we mentioned early in this book, recovery is the result of a series of small and correct action choices, taken in time, that help you discover what is emotionally unfinished for you. After discovery, there are the actions of completion. In the next chapter, we are going to tell you what the correct action choices are, demonstrate them from our own lives, and then help you take those actions.

6

THE RELATIONSHIP GRAPH

In chapter 4 we asked you to create a Pet Loss History Graph in order to see how you were affected and what you learned about dealing with loss. First we demonstrated ours and then showed you how to do it.

Now we're going to show you how to review and graph your relationship with one of your pets that died, with the goal of becoming emotionally complete with that pet. The review will help you recall the important events in your relationship with your pet, rather than just the general feeling of sadness that your pet is gone.

The purpose of the Relationship Graph is to help you move from discovery to completion. Creating the review is relatively easy although it may seem emotionally difficult to start. This is where you will need to reach down and find the courage to take this action. If not, you may stay stuck in your grief and stuck in the pain, which doesn't really honor your relationship with your pet. As before, we will demonstrate ours and then explain how to do it.

RUSSELL'S RELATIONSHIP GRAPH—BUDA

Russell's relationship with Buda begins with the dawn of the relationship (DOR), which was when he and Alice decided to get a dog. It's followed by other events Russell recalls from his relationship with Buda, with positive events above the line and negative events below the line. The events are close to chronological order, but may not be exact. We want you to know that it's not crucial that the dates or timeline be in perfect order. It's more important to remember the emotions attached to the events. As you'll see, although it was a glorious loving relationship, a great deal of emotion was generated by negative events and by the unexpected end of Buda's life.

Here is how Russell's relationship with Buda appears on his Relationship Graph.

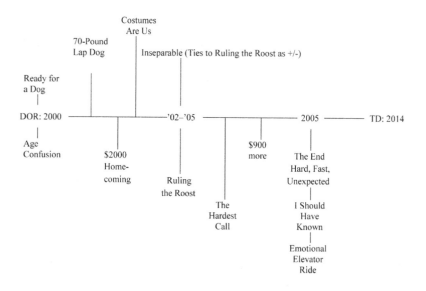

To help you see how this works, Russell wrote out a short narrative for each entry on his graph, which contained some of the details about the event and the emotions he had about them. As you read them, you'll see that it gives you a fairly clear picture about Russell's relationship with Buda.

Buda Relationship Narrative

LATE SEPTEMBER 2000

Dawn of the Relationship—Ready for a Dog: Alice and I decided we wanted a dog. I had my heart set on a Hungarian Vizsla. A friend knew of one who needed a home. We went and met Buda. It took us about an eighth of a second to fall in love with him.

Age Confusion: We were told that Buda was about eighteen months old, but the circumstances of his early life weren't known. In fact, he was probably at least five years old when we got him. This became very important later.

EARLY OCTOBER 2000–MARCH 2005

$2,000 Homecoming: On the day we got Buda, Alice and I left the house to go out for dinner. As novice pet owners, with no indication that Buda had major separation issues, we left him in the house. When we got back two hours and $2000 later, Buda had destroyed a sofa and a full set of wooden shutters. Apparently, feeling abandoned, he tried to claw his way out of the house. We felt terrible for Buda and the obvious level of fear that prompted him to panic. We also felt very naïve that we hadn't considered that a dog in a strange environment might be scared.

70-Pound Lap Dog: Buda was a muscular seventy pounds, but in his heart of hearts, he was a little guy who loved to curl up in my lap in front of the TV in my "grandpa" chair. My favorite photo is of the two of us asleep in that chair.

Costumes Are Us: Buda was incredibly patient with me, tolerating the costumes I subjected him to at Halloween. I dressed him up as Bozo the Pirate—wearing a giant bow tie and a black beanie with skull and crossbones and a rakish sash over one of his eyes. He brought joy to hundreds of kids at Halloween every year.

Ruling the Roost: Buda and I were inseparable. He came to work with me every day at The Grief Recovery Institute, and we went to the park every day to run and play. But as wonderful as my relationship with Buda was, there were problems. Since we weren't knowledgeable pet owners, we didn't know how to establish leadership. Sensing the void in leadership, Buda tried to rule the roost and caused some problems at the office. He nipped a few visitors and exhibited other dominant-aggressive behaviors.

The Hardest Call: After another incident, we decided we had to give Buda up. I called the friend who'd found Buda for us. He came to our condo to get Buda, but instead of just taking him, he asked us questions that led him to realize that we were the problem, not Buda. He helped us decide to keep Buda, but also taught us how to be better leaders. In retrospect, that day and the decision to keep Buda was one of the best ever.

$900 More: Another painful reminder of Buda's separation issues. One evening, I made a quick stop at a friend's house. I cracked the windows for Buda and went into the house. When I came back to the car, less than five minutes and $900 later, Buda had shredded the roof liner of the car in an attempt to claw his way out.

APRIL 2005

The End—Hard and Fast and Unexpected: On Sunday morning, April 10, Alice called me at my office to tell me Buda had vomited up his breakfast. I raced home. I sat at the piano bench and Buda came over and put his paws on my knees and licked my face—as if trying to tell me something. I took him to the vet immediately. When I told the vet that Buda was about six and a half years old, she looked at him and said he was probably much closer to ten than six. She took Buda for x-rays. When she came back, I knew—she didn't have to say anything. The x-rays revealed a virulent late-stage cancer and medical intervention wasn't feasible.

I Should Have Known: It was hard to believe it happened that fast, but I could see that Buda was different. The change in the last twenty-four hours was immense. It was obvious he was dying. As I talked with the vet, I said that I should have noticed something earlier. She helped by telling me about animals in general and dogs in particular, how they won't show weakness in the wild because it makes them vulnerable. She also mentioned that they can be very stoic about pain and discomfort. Even so, I had a hard time accommodating what was happening.

Emotional Elevator Ride: That Sunday was horrific, compounded by the fact that I was scheduled to fly to New York on Monday morning to appear on the *Today Show* on Tuesday. My anticipation about that appearance had been running high until Sunday, when it became almost irrelevant. All that mattered was Buda.

The next morning I sat in the departure lounge at LAX totally preoccupied with Buda, not knowing if he would be alive when I got back on Wednesday evening. I took out a legal pad and a pen and began reviewing my relationship with Buda. The words flew onto the paper—and so did the tears. I still have that tear-stained legal pad, so I can tell you that I started the graph at exactly 7:48 a.m. on April 11, 2005. The entries on the graph reflect what I wrote down that morning in the airport. The next few paragraphs represent things that happened over the next four days, and although they are not part of my original Relationship Graph, they are part of the completion communication I needed to make.

Not Nervous—Preoccupied: Tuesday morning at NBC in New York, I waited in the Green Room for my turn. It was a hectic morning as former President Clinton and California First Lady, Maria Schwarzenegger, were also on the show that day. Typically I would have been nervous, but I was so preoccupied with Buda that I wasn't worried about the interview.

Home Wednesday—Drained: I got home Wednesday evening, emotionally and physically exhausted. Buda was so sick he could hardly lift his head to greet me, but his tail thumped as much as it could. I got down on the floor and buried my face in his fur and sobbed. Alice and her daughter Claudia were there, sobbing in unison.

Buda's Last Hunt: With absolutely no hope of cure or abatement of his cancer, Alice and I had agreed not to go to any extraordinary measures to keep him alive. We didn't want to extend his life if he was to be in pain or discomfort. Thursday morning we had an appointment at the vet. That morning, prior to going to the vet, I took Buda one last time to the park on Hazeltine Avenue where he and I had spent so many happy hours.

The Longest Mile: It's about a mile from Hazeltine Park to the vet's office. It was a long, heartbreaking mile to drive knowing what was going to happen. The end was quick, and Buda didn't seem to suffer, just seemed to go to sleep. I stayed in the room for a while, then gave him a last hug and said my last good-bye. I can't remember much about the rest of that day except a lot of tears and how exceptionally sad I was that Buda was gone and we never got to go to the beach and so many other things I had hoped we would do together.

COLE'S RELATIONSHIP GRAPH—MAX

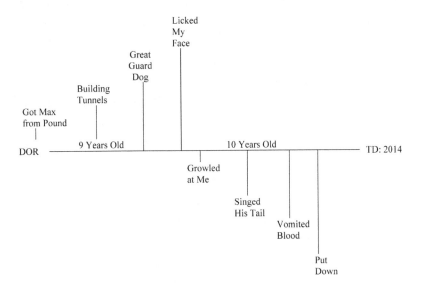

Max Relationship Narrative

9 Years Old—Got Max from the Pound: After Ninja ran away, my parents made sure *not* to teach me to *replace the loss*. They encouraged me to talk openly about my feelings, and they never told me I shouldn't feel the way I did. After some time, I felt ready to begin a relationship with another dog. We went to the pound and I found Max. He was a great-looking black Lab mix and very sweet.

9 Years Old—Helped Me Build Tunnels in Our Back Yard: Growing up, we had an area in our backyard that was all dirt. While my parents were deciding what to do with it, I got the go ahead to create a fort. As time went by, my friends and I decided we needed tunnels under the fort and with the help of Max, we spent hours digging. Often my friends would get tired and head home. Max and I would stay out there and put in a couple more hours. He was always by my side and a hard worker!

9 Years Old—Great Guard Dog, He Always Barked:
My dad had to travel often when I was young. Sometimes it was just my mom and me at the house. I always felt safe as long as Max was around. He had a great deep bark and was always alert to someone approaching our house. He was a big imposing dog and I always appreciated how seriously he took his job.

9 Years Old—Licked My face When I Came Home from Bad Days at School: He loved to lick my face and I loved having another furry friend. We had him for three years and he slept at the foot of my bed every night. We were best buddies! Whenever I came in the door, Max would rush to greet me and lick my face.

10 Years Old—Growled at Me: One day I came home from school and immediately knew something was not right. Max didn't greet me at the door—he just stood near the fireplace. I went over to greet him and he growled at me. That scared me, as he had never shown me anything but love.

10 Years Old—Singed His Tail Getting Away from Me: I went closer to him and he growled at me again and backed up into the fireplace, singeing his tail, and then ran into the back-yard. I started to cry. I knew something was very wrong. At that point, my mom heard the commotion and came into the living room. I told her what happened.

10 Years Old—Vomited Blood and Ultimately Had to Put Him Down: We found an overturned trash basket in our guest room where a friend of the family was staying. Max had gotten into some medication that our guest had thrown out. We called the vet, told him what was happening, and read him the label on the prescription bottle. He told us that there was nothing he could do for Max. He said Max would not make it, and in the meantime it would be excruciatingly painful. We went outside to find Max vomiting blood and trembling. I was terrified, unable to help the animal I loved so much. My mom called my dad and they realized we had to put Max out of his misery.

RELATIONSHIP GRAPH INSTRUCTIONS

Now that you've seen Russell's and Cole's Relationship Graphs, you have a good idea of how to do yours. As we move to the next action choice, we need to stop and help you consider which relationship you are going to graph. Most of you may choose to work on your relationship with your pet that died recently. Yet, because of the Pet Loss History you wrote, you may be aware that you have more than one incomplete relationship with pets that have died. If you feel compelled to go back and work on a pet that died some time ago, that's okay. After you have completed that one, you can work on the more current one and any others. In this exercise, you will only work on one relationship so you don't get them jumbled together. Once you've made your choice, you're ready to get to work.

Whether you're working on a very recent death or one from some time ago, it's most likely that the end of the physical part of your relationship with your pet is what brought you to this book. Up until now, you may have been focused on that ending. That makes sense because it's the last chapter of that relationship that is stored in your memory. However, you've probably also had flashes of memories of many other things that happened over the entire course of the relationship.

IN THE BEGINNING—
THE DAWN OF THE RELATIONSHIP

It's time to go back and look at the entire relationship, starting at the beginning. For most people, the relationship begins when they first see the puppy, kitten, or other animal that then becomes part of their life. However, for some people the relationship begins even before the first meeting. For them it begins with an idea or a dream of having a special relationship with an animal they haven't met yet.

You may recall how excited Cole was when his family was going to move and he could finally have a dog. Like many children, Cole had been begging his parents for a dog for a long time. The fact that his dream was finally going to come true was powerfully emotional for him.

For others, it's not even their own dream that creates the beginning of the relationship that winds up having such deep emotional impact on their lives. It's not uncommon for mom or dad—who merely goes along with getting a pet for their children—to wind up with a very powerful connection to the pet. In some situations, one spouse really wants the pet, but their mate winds up loving the pet just as much and is devastated when it dies. There are even times when people become temporary custodians of pets, and then, through circumstances, become the permanent guardians. People and animals being what they are, love can bloom from any kind of start.

No matter how or when your relationship with your pet began, we'll ask you to begin at your earliest memory of meeting or seeing the pet. We call that the dawn of the relationship, or DOR. From that starting place forward, we'll show you how to review the relationship and discover what were the most emotionally powerful and important things for you.

Note: As you start, we want to remind you that all relationships are unique, so husbands and wives who each had a relationship with their pet will naturally experience and attach different emotions to different events over the course of the relationship. The same is obviously true for brothers and sisters and any others who may have lived under a shared roof with a pet. With that in mind, we suggest that you not work together in taking these actions. That way the work you do will represent your unique emotional relationship with your pet.

For most people, the dawn of the relationship is the year in which they first saw the pet. Some people will remember the actual day and month of the first meeting. Those details are fine though not essential. Some of you may not actually know or remember the year. That's okay. The DOR is just the start point of the relationship.

The dawn of the relationship is often a chronicling date for other reasons as well. For some people, that date is also their birthday. For others, the pet was a wedding gift or a gift for some other special occasion. Allow the possibility that the DOR also encompasses other events that contain significant emotions for you. Since the essence of what we're doing here is addressing emotions, it's helpful to include any emotional connections that are meaningful for you.

When you're ready, set aside about an hour. All you need is two pieces of paper and pen or pencil. Have a box of tissues handy, just in case. This might be emotional for you.

CREATING YOUR RELATIONSHIP GRAPH— ACTION #4

You're almost ready to begin your Relationship Graph. But first, we're going to explain some of the details to help you set it up. Start by drawing a simple line across a piece of paper, with room above and below the line for dates and notes. You may need the second piece of paper for descriptive notes about the events you recall. Here's an example from someone whose relationship with their pet began in 2002. Now that you have awareness about the dawn of the relationship, you know that's where the graph will start.

DOR: 2002 ——————————————————————— TD: 2014

The dawn of the relationship (DOR) date goes at the left end of the line, and today's date (TD) goes at the right end. As we said earlier, you could put just the year or the actual date for the DOR. Today's date is the day you start the graph.

The DOR is not only the start date, but as we said, is possibly a date that has a great deal of emotional significance for you. A typical story is someone walking past cages of dogs, cats, or other animals in a pet store, or at a pet adoption event, or even crouched over a cardboard box at someone's home looking at a litter of puppies, kittens, mice, or whatever.

For many people, there's a magical moment when one of the animals catches their eye and wins their heart in an instant. Very often, that moment is the DOR moment for that person. It's the beginning of the relationship and the starting point of this set of actions you will take. There's a very high probability that your memory of that moment is a very sweet one, one that's liable to fill your face with a smile, even while it may bring tears to your eyes as you recall that first meeting. It's an excellent idea to note that moment on your graph. It goes above the line, and might look like this.

```
Pet Store
   |
  Eye
Contact
   |
 Heart
 Stolen
   |
DOR: 2002 ——————————————————————————————— TD: 2014
```

With those dates entered, you're ready to review your unique relationship with your pet. When you remember something and put it on the graph, make sure you use enough key words so you'll be able to understand what you meant later. The key words above the graph line—pet store, eye contact, heart stolen—are clear enough that you'd know what you were talking about.

You may be doing this exercise very shortly after the death of your pet, or it may be months or even years later. In any case, as you begin to write things down, you'll probably be flooded with memories of many events with your pet. For some of you, however, memories of specific events may not pop up as easily. To help you remember things that are important to you, we've prepared lists of general and specific categories that can act as a stimulus and a checklist for you to remember unique things about you and your pet.

GENERAL MEMORY CATEGORIES—CHECKLIST

- *Acquisition*
- *Behavior*
  - *Housebreaking*
  - *Training*
- *Grooming*
  - *Ticks, Fleas*
- *Veterinary Care and Other Health Issues*
- *Your Unique Friendship—The Communication Bond*
- *Other Friends*
  - *Housemates*
  - *Same Species*
  - *Other Animals*
  - *Humans*
- *Reproduction Issues*
  - *Joys and Problems*
  - *Litters or not*
- *Indoor*
- *Outdoor*
- *End-of-Life Issues—Care and Concern*
- *Memorials*

In addition to the general categories listed above, there are some specific events that are typical in many pet relationships. The following checklist will give you some reminders of the kind of events that may reflect many of your interactions with your pet. Of course, there can be many other events, but this list should allow your mind and heart to remember the most important things in your relationship. You'll notice that the first four entries relate to children who typically require adult permission to get a pet. It also gives us a chance to tell you that this graph is valuable for guiding you in helping your children deal with the deaths of their pets.

SPECIFIC MEMORY CATEGORIES—CHECKLIST

- *Getting Permission to Have a Pet*
- *Promising to Be Responsible For Care and Feeding*
- *Sleeping in the Child's Bed—Or Not*
- *Forgetting to Feed or Clean Up*
- *Hopes, Dreams, and Expectations*
- *Planning, Searching, and Finding the Pet*
- *The First Magical Moment or the First Conscious Memory*
- *Naming the Pet*
- *Early Traumas—Housebreaking, Crying All Night*
- *Scratching Furniture, Digging Holes*
- *Early Joys—Nuzzling, Playing*
- *Ran Away—Lost and Returned*
- *Table Manners—Begging and Eating "People" Food*
- *The Bond of Trust—Best Friends—No Secrets*
- *Feeling Loved and Supported at Difficult Times*
- *Indoor—Outdoor; Possible Source of Pain about the Death*
- *Fighting with Other Animals—Protecting the Yard*
- *Times at the Park*

- *Friendly to House Guests—Or Not*
- *Trips to the Vets*
- *Regarding Long-Term Illness:*
  - *Getting Sick—Diagnosis, Treatment, and Medications*
  - *Pain and Frustration of Watching Illness*
  - *The Decision to Put the Pet to "Sleep"*
- *The Last Day*

REVIEWING THE RELATIONSHIP

Start reviewing your relationship with your pet on your graph. Put positive events and memories above the line and negative events below the line. As we've indicated, our relationships with our pets tend to be predominantly good, so many of your entries will be above the line and only a few will go below. However, please be alert that you may have more negative and painful events near the end of your pet's life.

Also, you may have more memories about the feelings you have about your pet than you do about specific events. It's perfectly okay to put those feelings as entries on your graph. For example, you may have felt that your pet was the only entity you could trust with your innermost thoughts and feelings, sometimes about people you were struggling with. You can put that above the line with a note—*safe to trust with my feelings*. As an example, here is that idea as the second entry after the DOR on the graph:

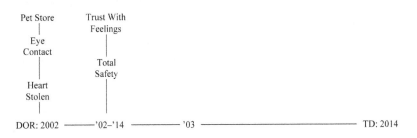

Notice that the dates on this entry indicate that the sense of emotional safety with the pet ran through the entire time of the relationship: '02–'14. That's very common, and may be true for you also. If not, put the date or dates that reflect the truth as you remember it.

The next event you recall might have been scary. If the pet had run out of the house and into the street, it would go on the graph below the line, with a note about how terrified you were. Clearly that would be one of the less-than-positive events in your relationship with your pet. But in creating this graph, it's essential that we have all the major elements, good, bad, and sometimes ugly. It would look like this:

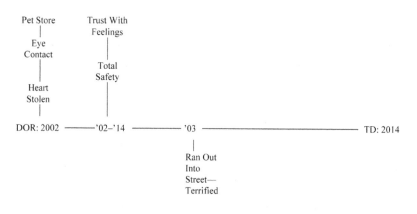

Let's say that your pet is a dog and that your next memory is of the first of hundreds of hikes in the hills, with the pup running ahead, sniffing everything, and running back to you to report his findings. As you think about those hikes and the incredible feeling of oneness with your dog and with nature, your heart fills. As you can imagine, that goes above the line. You would put it on the graph with a note: hikes, nature, connection. It would look like this:

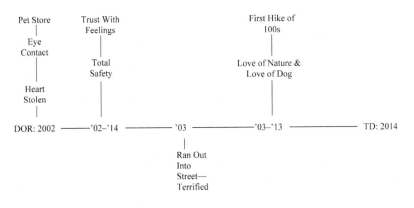

What we've done with the dates is show that the first hike was in 2003, when the pup was about a year old, and the hikes went on for the next ten years. If there were some extraordinary events on some of those other hikes, they would get their own entry with a note. An example might be the first time he chased a rabbit, or was scared by a coyote. The event would be either above or below the line or, in some cases, both above and below. An example of both might be the first time you let your dog off the leash and he took off, which scared you, but when you called and whistled, he came back to you. Many events might be both positive and negative, above and below the line. If the hikes stopped when he got older and his hips couldn't take the hills anymore, that might have its own entry since that will have some emotional content for you.

(Although we're using events with a dog companion to demonstrate the graph, the same ideas apply with most pets. Training and riding a horse may have different elements than those with dogs or cats, but we know there's a tremendous amount of emotion connected with all human to animal relationships.)

Now that you have the idea, continue using the general and specific lists we provided, along with your own recollections, to think of things that are important to you in your relationship with your pet—all the things you used to do with them are part of your grief as you learn to adapt to your life without them. Please don't omit something because you think it small or insignificant. If it comes into your mind—or heart—put it on your graph.

You do not have to create a narrative. In our examples we wrote the graph entries out in long form. As long as you are clear about the event and emotions, you have what you need to move to the next set of actions. However, if you wish to write them out, that's okay too.

No matter if you finished your Relationship Graph yet or not, we want to congratulate you for having the courage to do this work.

7

CONVERTING YOUR RELATIONSHIP GRAPH INTO RECOVERY CATEGORIES

At many levels, our relationships with our pets are simple and straightforward, while at the same time being incredibly emotional. In order to keep moving toward the goal of completion, you must convert the entries on your Relationship Graph into categories that will help you complete what you've discovered. Fortunately, there are only three categories:

- Apologies
- Forgiveness
- Significant Emotional Statements

Before we start helping you convert your graph into the three recovery categories, we're going to give you brief explanations about each of them. The aim is to help you achieve completion of anything that was left emotionally incomplete at the time of the pet's death, or since. Generally, because the relationships with our pets are less complicated, the kinds of things we need to apologize for or forgive are different from those in our human relationships. We'll explain how to communicate anything that falls into these categories.

APOLOGIES

We use the most basic definition of "apology" from *Merriam-Webster: a statement saying that you are sorry about something: an expression of regret for having done or said something wrong.* An apology can be for something you did, or for something you didn't do. An example of the first would be, "I'm sorry I yelled at you when I was cranky. I know you only wanted to please me and you didn't understand my anger." An example of something you didn't do that you might need to apologize for would be, "I always planned to take you to the beach to run. I thought you'd love that. I'm sorry that I never followed through on that plan."

FORGIVENESS MAY BE MORE COMPLICATED

Forgiveness can be more complicated because so many people mix forgiveness up with the idea that it excuses bad behavior. When they do that, they become totally unable (or unwilling) to forgive. Without forgiveness, they carry the hurt and resentment forward, even after the animal—or person—who hurt or offended them has died. Again, even though our relationships with our pets are less complicated than with people, there are almost always a few things we need to forgive them for. The absence of forgiveness can keep us stuck and emotionally incomplete.

We use the dictionary definition of "forgive," which is: *to cease to feel resentment against (an offender).* The idea that the offender is parenthetical can be a major key to helping you realize that forgiveness is for you, not the other being, whether animal or human. The action of stating the forgiveness in a way we'll show you allows you to accomplish the goal of ceasing to feel the resentment you've been harboring.

Forgiveness and apologies share a basic idea. They may need to be issued for things that happened or didn't happen. In the apology section we explained that you can issue apologies for things you did, and for things you didn't do. The same holds true for forgiveness. Here is an example of something the pet may have done: "I forgive you for chewing up my very expensive shoes." Or an example for a nonevent: "I forgive you for never wanting to play fetch or Frisbee."

Holding on to your anger or resentment can't hurt an animal that has died—it can only hurt you. But even with that idea and the accurate and helpful dictionary definition, many people fight forgiveness. In order to help even more, we suggest adding a simple phrase at the end of the forgiveness, so now it would read like this: "I forgive you for chewing up my very expensive shoes. *I forgive you so I can be free.*"

In spite of the above, there are still people who just can't get past the idea that forgiveness somehow excuses bad behavior. If you're still stuck, we offer a definition we created years ago, and which appears in all our books. Our unique definition is: "I acknowledge the thing you did—or did not do—that hurt me, and I'm not going to let my memory of that event hurt me anymore." Since our animals rarely do anything with real intent to harm us, we doubt you'll need that definition, but if you struggle with the idea of forgiveness, it can help you get unstuck.

Note: If you are harboring a significant amount of resentment, anger, or frustration toward another person—either living or dead—we encourage you to get a copy of *The Grief Recovery Handbook*. Read it and take the actions it outlines for dealing with any incompleteness you have with them.

FORGIVENESS IS AN ACTION NOT A FEELING

We have touched on the fact that grieving pet owners are sometimes stuck on elements of their story that relate to veterinarians and their staffs. They often hold a great deal of resentment about misdiagnosis, treatment, medications, and more. Many of those people who tell their story in an endless loop are stuck on these topics that keep them away from the primary issues, which are the death of their pet and their relationship with the pet that died. They wind up devoting a tremendous amount of emotional energy to the vet or vet techs or others, and not very much to their pet. One of the reasons they stay stuck is because they are focused on those people or organizations and not on their pet.

In order to help them, we suggest that they forgive those people who they believe did wrong or bad things. The forgiveness allows them to focus on the death of their pet instead of those people. We are not saying that by forgiving someone, you are giving up your right to sue them if they did something illegal. We are just giving you the ability to work on your relationship with your pet that died, which is the cause of your broken heart.

The same is true if your pet was killed in a hit-and-run by a car. If you stay focused on the driver of the car, you are removed from what you need to do in relationship to your pet that died. You must forgive the perpetrator so you can deal with your broken heart. Again, if the perpetrator can be found and brought to justice, your forgiveness doesn't mean that you don't press charges. We've known too many people who stay focused on the driver and not on their pet. Forgiveness is your key to the emotional freedom you need to deal with your loss.

When we suggest forgiveness, many people tell us they don't "feel" it. We agree. Forgiveness is an action not a feeling. It is not natural to want to forgive or to feel forgiveness of those we believe have hurt us. But if you hold on to the resentment you feel, you are not free. You give your power away and it *keeps you from your primary issue, which is about your pet that died.*

If nothing else, remember this phrase: "I forgive you so I can be free."

SIGNIFICANT EMOTIONAL STATEMENTS

Significant Emotional Statements are exactly what you might guess they are. They are things you need to say that are important to you but are neither apologies nor forgiveness. A few simple examples that relate to your pet might be: "I loved you more than I can even say." "I felt so safe and trusting with you." "I was always amazed at how gentle you could be with little children." "Thank you for greeting me like a conquering hero when I got home from work every day; that made me feel like a million dollars every time."

As you can see, those statements are exactly what we said, they are significant and they are emotional. And, as we've indicated, you may have a great many statements that you'll need and want to make under that heading. Even though you probably told your pet "I love you" many times, in the context of this work, that statement will take on added significance.

Many people simply feel cheated out of the opportunity to say things one more time, especially "I love you" and "Goodbye." The Significant Emotional Statement category gives you a chance to say anything important to you, whether you never said it before or if you'd said it many times. The same is true for many other comments that you may or may not have made to your pet. It is really helpful to say them or repeat them as you take these actions.

Here are a few more important pieces of guidance. The first is that any negative Significant Emotional Statement must be accompanied by a forgiveness. If not, you keep the unfinished business associated with the negative events. For example, if you say, "I hated that you didn't come when I called and it always scared me that you would get hurt," you leave the feeling of hating open. You can correct that simply by adding, "and I forgive you so I can be free."

The second guideline is about something that's not very likely to occur in your relationship with your pet, but we'll explain it just in case you run into it. For example, some grievers, when talking about a parent with whom they had a rocky relationship, will want to say, "He did the best he could with what he had to work with." Almost without exception people say that knowing that their parent(s) had a really tough time in their own childhood. The problem is that the statement wipes out any and all forgiveness they may have issued about the negative or painful things their parent did to them. It also inadvertently condones the bad things rather than forgiving them.

Before we suggest an alternative to "You did the best you could," we ask the person if she or he has any compassion for the parent (or other person) they're working on. If they say yes, then we offer them what we think is a better way to communicate that compassion. "Dad, I have compassion for you and the things that happened to you early in your life." That way they get to make that statement, if it's true for them, without wiping out the meaning and value of the forgiveness they issued earlier.

As we said, it's not too likely to be a scenario with your pet, but it is possible. Quite often when we've adopted pets that had troublesome early lives that we can't really ever know about, they do things that are difficult to live with. Cole rescued a dog, George, with massive separation anxiety issues. George can never be left alone, and it alters the lives of everyone connected to the family. They each need to forgive George for the things they have to do to work around his problem of being alone. At the same time, they have compassion for George and the likelihood that he was separated too early from his dam and his littermates. In doing a completion, after issuing the forgiveness, they would each say much the same as was mentioned above, "George, I have compassion for you and whatever happened to make you so frightened of being alone."

FORGIVENESS IN DAY-TO-DAY LIVING WITH OUR PETS

Forgiveness is not limited to communications that need to be made after a pet dies.

We mentioned above that Cole and his family have needed to forgive George because of the inconveniences caused by his separation anxiety. George is a young, vital dog who has some emotional baggage, like many of us do.

Animals can have fears that affect how they behave, but there isn't always an effective way to help them change those behaviors. Since change isn't always possible, it is important for each of us to master the moment-to-moment skill of forgiveness so we don't build up resentments against the pets we love.

RECAPPING THE CATEGORIES

It may seem simplistic that there are only three categories needed to complete anything that you discover to be incomplete for you in your relationship with your pet that died. But we assure you that anything of emotional value to you can be communicated within one or more of those three categories.

Notice we just said "anything of emotional value to you." It's important that you not complicate this process by getting analytical, intellectual, or philosophical. Just focus on what is emotionally true for you.

CONVERTING RUSSELL'S RELATIONSHIP GRAPH INTO RECOVERY CATEGORIES

In the last chapter, we showed you Russell's graph of his relationship with Buda. We're going to repeat some of the entries here, only this time, at the end of each paragraph, you'll see a comment in bold print which represents the conversion of the content of the graph into the recovery categories, Apologies **[A]**, Forgiveness **[F]**, and Significant Emotional Statements **[SES]**.

$2000 Homecoming: On the day we got Buda, Alice and I left the house to go out for dinner. As novice pet owners, with no indication that Buda had major separation issues, we left him in the house. When we got back two hours and $2000 later, Buda had destroyed a sofa and a full set of wooden shutters. Apparently, feeling abandoned, he tried to claw his way out of the house. We felt terrible for Buda and the obvious level of fear that prompted him to panic. We also felt very naïve that we hadn't considered that a dog in a strange environment might be scared. **I needed to apologize to Buda for leaving him alone and forgive him for the damage he did. [A & F = Apology & Forgiveness]**

70-Pound Lap Dog: Buda was a muscular seventy pounds, but in his heart of hearts, he was a little guy who loved to curl up in my lap in front of the TV in my "grandpa" chair. My favorite photo is of the two of us asleep in the chair. **I needed to thank**

him for all the sweet memories. [SES = Significant Emotional Statement]

Costumes Are Us: Buda was incredibly patient with me, tolerating the costumes I subjected him to at Halloween. I dressed him up as Bozo the Pirate—wearing a giant bow tie and a black beanie with skull and crossbones and a rakish sash over one of his eyes. He brought joy to hundreds of kids at Halloween every year. **I needed to apologize for robbing him of his hunting dog dignity and thank him for being such a good sport.** [A & SES]

Ruling The Roost: Buda and I were inseparable. He came to work with me every day at The Grief Recovery Institute. But as wonderful as my relationship with Buda was, there were problems. Since we weren't knowledgeable pet owners, we didn't know how to establish leadership. Sensing the void in leadership, Buda tried to rule the roost and caused some problems at the office. He nipped a few visitors and exhibited other dominant-aggressive behaviors. This is an example of a memory that belongs both above and below the line. **I needed to apologize to Buda for me not being a good leader and forgive him for the aggressive things he did.** [A & F]

The Hardest Call: After another incident, we decided we had to give Buda up. I called the friend who'd found Buda for us. He came to our condo to get Buda, but instead of just taking him, he asked us questions that led him to realize that we were the problem, not Buda. He helped us decide to keep Buda, but also learn how to be better leaders. In retrospect, that day and that decision was one of the best ever. **I needed to tell Buda how much I loved him and that we just couldn't let him go.** [SES]

$900 More: Another painful reminder of Buda's separation issues. One evening, I made a quick stop at a friend's house. I cracked the windows for Buda and went into the house. When I came back to the car, less than five minutes and $900 later, Buda had shredded the roof liner of the car in an attempt to claw his way out. **I needed to apologize for leaving him in the car and for the way I yelled at him; and I needed to forgive him for the damage he did.** [A & F]

The End—Hard and Fast and Unexpected: On Sunday morning, April 10, 2005, Alice called me at my office to tell me Buda had vomited up his breakfast. I raced home. I sat at the piano bench and Buda came over and put his paws on my knees and licked my face—as if trying to tell me something. I took him to the vet immediately. When I told the vet that Buda was about six and a half years old, she said he was probably much closer to ten than six. She took Buda for x-rays. When she came back, I knew—she didn't have to say anything. The x-rays revealed a virulent late-stage cancer and medical intervention wasn't feasible. **I needed to tell Buda how sad I was that nothing could be done to save him.** [SES]

I Should Have Known: It was hard to believe it happened that fast, but I could see that Buda was different. The change in the last twenty-four hours was immense. It was obvious he was dying. As I talked with the vet, I said that I should have noticed something earlier. She helped by telling me about animals in general and dogs in particular, how they won't show weakness in the wild because it makes them vulnerable, and that they can be very stoic about pain and discomfort. Even so, I had a hard time accommodating what was happening. **I needed to tell Buda how sorry I was if there were signs I should have seen earlier.** [A]

Emotional Elevator Ride: That Sunday was horrific, compounded by the fact that I was scheduled to fly to New York on Monday morning, to appear on the *Today Show* on Tuesday. My anticipation about that appearance had been running high until Sunday, when it became almost irrelevant. **I needed to tell Buda how hard it was for me to leave him.** [SES]

Not Nervous—Preoccupied: Tuesday morning at NBC, I waited in the Green Room for my turn. It was a hectic morning as former President Clinton and California First Lady, Maria Schwarzenegger, were also there. Typically I would have been nervous, but I was so preoccupied with Buda, I wasn't worried about the interview. **I needed to tell Buda that I dedicated that show to him.** [SES]

Home Wednesday—Drained: I got home Wednesday evening, emotionally and physically exhausted. Buda was so sick he could hardly lift his head to greet me, but his tail thumped as much as it could. I got down on the floor and buried my face in his fur and sobbed. Alice and her daughter Claudia were there. I took out the tear-stained legal pad with the graph and letter I'd written Monday morning at the airport. (We'll introduce and explain the letter in the next chapter.) The three of us gathered around Buda's bed. I read the letter to Buda—as best I could—with tears streaming down my face. Alice and Claudia sobbed in unison. **I wanted Buda to hear me telling him all the things I needed to say.** [SES]

Buda's Last Hunt*: With absolutely no hope of cure or abatement of his cancer, Alice and I had agreed not to go to any extraordinary measures to keep him alive. We didn't want to extend his life if he was to be in pain or discomfort. Thursday morning we had an appointment at the vet. That morning, prior to going to the vet, I took Buda one last time to the park on Hazeltine Avenue where he and I had spent so many happy hours. **I wanted him to have one last time at our park.** [SES]

(*That visit to the park is detailed in an e-mail I sent to John called "Buda's Last Hunt," which is reprinted in chapter 8.)

The Longest Mile: It's about a mile from Hazeltine Park to the vet's office. It was a long, heartbreaking mile to drive knowing what was going to happen. The end was quick, and Buda didn't seem to suffer; he just appeared to go to sleep. I stayed in the room for a while, then gave him a last hug and said my last good-bye. I can't remember much about the rest of that day except a lot of tears, and how exceptionally sad I was that he never got to go to the beach and so many other things I had hoped we would do together. **I needed to tell him how sad I was and how much I missed him.** [SES]

IDENTIFYING YOUR RECOVERY CATEGORIES—ACTION #5

Now it's your turn to convert your Relationship Graph into the recovery categories. Set aside about an hour. You need your graph and a pen, and a box of tissues, just in case. It may be emotional for you as you go over the relationship with your pet.

Look at each entry on your graph and decide which category or categories it falls into. If you're not sure how to do it, go back and look at Russell's example. You'll see that several of the events have more than one recovery category. That's very common. You can use the same abbreviations, A = Apologies, F = Forgiveness, SES = Significant Emotional Statements. If you do that you can enter them right on the graph. Or you can take a separate piece of paper and list the events from the graph and then put the category letter or letters next to them. Using one of Russell's entries, it would look like this:

> **$900 More:** I needed to apologize for leaving him in the car and for the way I yelled at him; and I needed to forgive him for the damage he did. [**A** & **F**]

Be patient and gentle with yourself as you do this. The amount of effort and emotional truth you put into this will be valuable for you when we get to the next action.

8

THE GRIEF RECOVERY METHOD COMPLETION LETTER©

Having taken all the actions suggested in this book so far, you are now ready to take action to complete the loss. Since your pet died, you have probably become familiar with the pain associated with it. Now is the time to complete your relationship with that pain by completing what is unfinished between you and your pet.

Again, we want to emphasize that feeling incomplete is normal and natural as our minds and hearts go over all the things we wish had been different, better, or more; and all the unrealized hopes, dreams, and expectations we had about the future. We also want to remind you that even though you probably said "I love you" and other emotionally important statements many times directly to your pet, it's time to put them and a host of other statements together in the context of a special completion communication.

PROPER CONTENT LEADS TO COMPLETION

Misinformation is the major stumbling block to completion. We know that many people, at the suggestion of well-meaning friends or professionals, write farewell letters to their pets that have died. Writing a farewell letter, without proper content, is another piece of misinformation. The origin of the concept of writing a farewell letter is buried in antiquity. Over time, farewell letters have lost their primary motive regarding completion. Sadly, now they often are simply a painful recitation of events and emotions, much like a newsletter. People who have written such letters report a measure of short-term relief, but no long-term benefit.

Invariably, people wrote those farewell letters without taking the actions outlined in this book. Those attempts are unsuccessful because they lack the proper content, which is achieved by creating a Relationship Graph and then converting it into the three recovery categories: Apologies, Forgiveness, and Significant Emotional Statements.

You're about to write what we call a Grief Recovery Method Completion Letter, which is similar in some ways to what is called a farewell letter. But there are some major differences, the most important being that the letter must contain the "proper content" to help you accomplish the goal of feeling emotionally complete. Proper content is the result of the discovery work you've been doing in the exercises in this book.

In order to be successful and to create a sense of completion, it is now essential that you convert all the prior work you have done into a *completion* letter rather than a *farewell* letter or newsletter.

The effective completion letter you write will help you achieve the three goals we outlined for you early in this book:

- To have fond memories of your relationship with your pet not turn painful
- To be able to remember your pet the way you know him in life, not only as in death
- To have a life of meaning and value, even though your life will be different

As in the previous actions, we will first demonstrate then explain how to write your letter.

RUSSELL'S COMPLETION LETTER TO BUDA

Dearest Buda,

I have been reviewing our relationship and have discovered some things I want to say.

Buda, when I first saw you, I knelt down to pet you and you immediately turned and put your butt in my lap—a technique I later learned you used with everybody—but in that moment, you had me, I was yours.

I remember with horror that first evening we left you in the house and you destroyed the shutters and sofa. We didn't know you'd have such a reaction to being left alone. Alice was so upset that I was afraid we'd have to give you back. Buda, I'm sorry we left you alone, and I forgive you for destroying the shutters and the sofa.

Alice and I weren't really dog people and bad things happened because we didn't know how to be "pack leaders." You tried to run our house and our lives—a job you were ill equipped for. Buda, I'm sorry we didn't know how to be the leaders. You became dominant-aggressive and even bit a few people. Buda, I forgive you for those incidents.

Finally, we felt no alternative but to give you back. With heavy hearts, we called Bobby to come get you. We stood on the corner with you and Bobby for almost two hours. In the end, we just couldn't let you go. Instead Bobby taught me how to train you. As I learned how to lead, you got more and more comfortable. The aggressive behavior disappeared and we could trust you anywhere. I am eternally grateful that we didn't give you back. Buda, I wouldn't trade my time with you for anything in the world—thank you!

So much of what I recall relates to our time at the park. I remember the time you were sitting there in your regal splendor and a little girl and her mother passed by. The little girl said, "Mommy, look at that dog, he has such wonderful posture." I was so proud of you!

Best of all are all the times I'd watch you holding a point on a covey of birds. It was magical. You were like a canine version of Marcel Marceau, with body movements so small and precise I almost couldn't tell that you were moving at all. Since I wasn't a hunter, you never really got to hunt. Buda, I'm sorry for that, but I'm thrilled you had those times in the park and got to be what you were born to be, a hunting dog.

Thinking of our hours in the park, I remember the pleasure of watching your incredible athleticism and grace. Buda, thanks for all that joy and pride I felt. And thanks for the whole new group of four-legged and two-legged friends we met at the park.

Although our lives together got better and better, your old fears never went completely away. I remember stopping by Deb's house and leaving you in the car for just a few minutes. When I came back, $900 later, you had destroyed the roof liner trying to claw your way out. I guess your past still haunted you. Buda, I'm sorry I left you in the car. I apologize for yelling and using curse words you'd never heard before. And Buda, I forgive you for wrecking the inside of the car.

Buda, your presence at the Grief Recovery Institute as mascot, guard dog, and touchstone was a constant joy to me and to others. Thank you—I'll never forget the way you'd lick away people's tears when they cried.

Thanks for putting up with me dressing you up for Halloween and Fourth of July. You were a good sport. Buda, I'm sorry if that robbed you of your dignity as a hunting dog, but I think you liked all the attention you got.

One of my fondest memories is of the two of us asleep in my grandpa chair. The connection I felt to you is overwhelmingly emotional even now. Buda, I'm particularly sorry for the last few times I said no when you wanted to get into the chair with me. If I had known what was going to happen . . . I would have done it differently.

Last Sunday, the fateful Sunday of your diagnosis, I was at the office when Alice called and told me you'd vomited up your breakfast. I raced home, sensing that something was terribly wrong. When I got home, I sat on the piano bench and you came over to me and put your paws on my knees and with great effort, stood up and licked my face. It was a magical but painful moment, as if you were trying to tell me something. The speed at which you had deteriorated, without any apparent symptoms, was unbelievable. When the vet told me you had an untreatable cancer, I was devastated. She said you could be kept alive for a short while, but there was no hope of you getting better. Buda, I couldn't imagine you not being able to run and hunt, nor could I imagine you just lying on your bed waiting to die.

As you and I sat in that little room at the vet's, waiting for Alice so she could talk to the vet and participate in the decisions we had to make, my mind raced to the things we never got to do like go to the beach and hike in the mountains. Buda, I'm sorry that you never got to do those things. But I'm glad we went to the park every day, for years, and that we risked Alice's wrath for muddying up the carpet upon our return on rainy days.

Buda, I'm so sad that your life got cut short. I'm so sorry that I couldn't see or prevent what happened. I'll never forget the last morning of your life, The Last Hunt. It reminds me of the thousands of hours of companionship we had, and how my *relationship with you expanded all my relationships—thank you Buda.*

Buda, I will dedicate my appearance on the Today Show *to you, in my heart, if not in words. And you can bet there will someday be a book and this letter will be a part of it. Even then, you'll be helping so many people deal with their broken hearts about their companions who died.*

One last thing, sweet boy. I remember all the times I'd come home and your entire body would wiggle with excitement like you couldn't contain yourself. That gave me such a feeling of acceptance and affection. Buda, thank you for those magical moments, and so much more. I will never forget them.

I love you.

I miss you.

Good-bye, Buda

Russell's letter is long and very thorough. We reprinted it here in its entirety so you could see how he combined the entries from his graph and the categories to create the letter. Since it covers a wide variety of events, it may help you with your letter. You'll also notice that there are a few things in the letter that are not on the Relationship Graph. They are emotional things that came to Russell as he was writing the letter. One of them is about their first meeting when Buda nestled into Russell's lap; another is the story about the little girl talking about Buda's posture; and one more is Russell's memory of hours in the grandpa chair.

You may have things that come up as you write your letter. It's perfectly okay to put them in. Be careful though not to turn it into a newsletter. Anything you put in the letter still needs to come under the heading of one or more of the three recovery categories. When Russell wrote about the little girl he said: *So much of what I recall relates to our time at the park. I remember the time you were sitting there in your regal splendor and a little girl and her mother passed by. The little girl said, "Mommy, look at that dog, he has such wonderful posture." I was so proud of you!* The significant emotional statement is "I was so proud of you."

COLE'S COMPLETION LETTER TO MAX

Dear Max,

I have been reviewing our relationship and have discovered some things that I want to tell you.

Max, thank you for helping me build that intricate "tunnel system" in the backyard. We spent hours doing that and I always loved your company.

Max, thanks for always protecting me. You had a great bark and I always felt safe when I went to sleep knowing that you were there. I apologize for never telling you what that meant to me.

Max, even when I came home from school and I got a bad note from the teacher, you were always there wagging your tail and licking my face. You loved to give kisses and I loved getting them.

Max, I was so scared when you growled at me. I was confused and knew something was very wrong.

Max, I am so sorry that our friend left those pills where you could get them.

Max, the image of you singeing your tail in the fireplace when you were trying to get away from me is very painful. I have to let go of the pain now.

Max, it broke my heart to see you in so much pain. You looked so scared and all I wanted to do was help you but I couldn't. I have to let go of the pain so I can be free.

*Max, I want you to know that we only wanted to stop
your suffering when we put you down. The vet told us that you
weren't going to make it and you would have had a lot of pain
and suffering.*

*Max, I feel robbed of a lot of years together as best buddies.
You were such a sweet, energetic pup and I have to let go of the
pain now so that I can be free.*

I miss you. I love you. Good-bye Max.

You'll notice that Russell's and Cole's letters are different in
style and length, but they are similar in the format to make sure
that they communicate what is emotionally true for each of them.
Your letter will be unique to you and will reflect the one-of-a-
kind relationship you had with your pet.

WRITING YOUR GRIEF RECOVERY METHOD COMPLETION LETTER—ACTION #6

Your completion letter will help you become emotionally complete with everything about your relationship with your pet that
has been unfinished until now. The letter allows you to keep fond
memories and all positive aspects of the relationship. You can also
keep your beliefs about heaven and other spiritual principles.

You will now be able to say good-bye to what is incomplete. You will be able to say good-bye to any pain you associate
with this relationship including any unmet hopes, dreams, and
expectations. It is most important that you remember that good-
bye signals the end of this communication—*it is not the end of the
relationship*. Remember we said that the emotional and spiritual
aspects of relationships continue for us after our pets have died.

It is finally time to write your completion letter. We don't want this letter to be an unsuccessful attempt at recovery for you. It's not a good idea to discuss what you're doing with others. Friends and relatives may mean well, but they haven't read what you've read. They haven't done the work you've done. Please pay close attention to these instructions on how to say what is most important for you.

General Instruction: Writing the letter is best done alone, and in one complete session. Writing the letter can be an emotionally painful experience, and there is too much temptation to avoid the pain. You've already proven your courage. Use it now to write this letter. You may have sensed that there were some things that weren't emotionally complete, but you just didn't know what to do about it.

Specific Instructions: Allow at least an hour, and as always, have some tissues handy. The most effective way to write your letter is to have your Relationship Graph and your lists of Apologies, Forgiveness, and Significant Emotional Statements in front of you. Look over the review and the lists and then write your letter. Your graph and lists may contain many repetitions. It is not necessary to repeat the same recovery communications over and over. Use this letter to consolidate them into the most concise expression possible. Your letter should be primarily focused on the recovery categories.

There is no limit on how much you can write, but the emotional intensity is often lost in volume. This is your opportunity to say the most important unsaid things—but it is okay to repeat significant things you'd said to your pet, like "I love you," and other meaningful comments. Generally, two or three standard pages are sufficient. It is okay to write a little more or a little less. If you write more than five pages, you probably need to consider whether you've turned it into a newsletter or if you are repeating the same things.

Writing the letter may or may not be an emotional experience for you. Do not be concerned if it is not emotional. Every griever is different and unique.

Here is a helpful format for your letter:

Dear Buda,
I have been reviewing our relationship and I discovered some
    things that I want to tell you.
Buda, I apologize for . . .
Buda, I apologize for . . .
Buda, I apologize for . . .
*(You may have only one or two communications in this section, or you may
    have more.)*
Buda, I forgive you for . . .
Buda, I forgive you for . . .
Buda, I forgive you for . . .
*(Again, you may have only one or two communications in this section, or
    you may have more.)*
Buda, I want you to know . . . (significant emotional statement)
Buda, I want you to know . . . (significant emotional statement)
Buda, I want you to know . . . (significant emotional statement)
(You will probably have several communications in this section.)

The above is a general format for your letter. It is not essential that you begin with apologies, or that you group the communications by category. As you noticed in Russell's letter, several of his completion statements were a mixture of apologies and forgiveness, or forgiveness and significant emotional statements. Also, it's a good idea to start most of your statements with your pet's name, or use the name within the statement. It may help you access your emotions as you write and later when you read your letter.

CLOSING YOUR LETTER

In order to complete what you have discovered, you must end your letter effectively. When you speak to a friend on the phone, you conclude the conversation with the word "good-bye," to signal the end of that conversation. We conclude our completion letter with good-bye to signal the end of this communication.

For the vast majority of grieving people, the most effective and accurate closing is simply: "I love you. I miss you. Good-bye, Buda." We are not saying this is the only correct ending for your letter, but it tends to be accurate for most people. There are other options based on your unique relationship with your pet. What should remain constant are the very last words, "Good-bye," and the name of your pet. Failure to say good-bye can often negate all the good work you've done. *It is the good-bye that completes the communication.* Do not substitute other words. Not saying good-bye leaves the communication open and runs the risk of leaving you incomplete.

It is rare, though not impossible, for a grieving pet owner to write a completion letter and not feel as if the statements *I love you* and *I miss you* are accurate for them. But if those are not truthful for you, do not say them. An effective alternate is, "I have to go now, and I have to let go of the pain—Good-bye, Buda." Generally, that's only liable to be true if you did not have a positive and loving relationship with your pet and that the relationship itself was difficult or painful for you.

READING YOUR GRIEF RECOVERY METHOD COMPLETION LETTER—ACTION #7

Now that you've written your completion letter there is one more action to take. You may recall that Russell read his completion letter to Buda the night before Buda died, with Alice and Claudia listening. The circumstances that allowed that to happen were probably different than your situation. There is a high probability that your pet has already died by the time you get to this book and write this letter.

The reading of the letter with a human witness is essential for you to have a sense of completion. The important detail for Russell is that there were human witnesses. Although the graph and the letter itself represent your emotional truth about your relationship with your pet, it is the reading of the letter with a witness that gives you a sense of being heard. That is a major aspect of what creates the feeling of emotional completion. We can't tell you exactly why this is true, but we know from many people who've written letters to pets or people but didn't have a human witness that they didn't have the sense of completion.

The question now is, who should you choose to listen as you read your letter? The keys to that answer are safety, trust, and lack of judgment. You need to choose someone who covers those three areas so you will feel free to be emotional (or not) as you read your letter.

It's important that the listener be in the same room with you as you read your letter. We do not recommend that you read your letter to your listener over the phone or via Skype.

We want this last piece of the puzzle to be effective for you, so we're going to give instructions for your listener, as well as letter reading instructions for you.

Instructions for the Listener

1. Your first instruction is to adopt the image of a *heart with ears*. It is your job to listen and listen only. You may laugh or cry if appropriate, but *you must not talk at all*. Nothing about what you do can imply judgment, criticism, or analysis.

2. Take a position at least a few feet away from the reader. We don't want you in their face, as it can be a little intimidating. Let your body be relaxed. Do not have pen or paper in your hands. You are a friend listening to an important communication.

3. During the letter reading, do not touch the reader at all. At this juncture, touch usually stops feelings. We want to allow this reading to be emotional if that should happen. The reader will have their own tissues handy.

4. There is a very real possibility that you might be affected by listening to what your friend reads. Please let that be okay with you. However, you must keep in mind that this is not about you, so to a limited degree you have to control the intensity of your reaction. On the other hand, if tears sprout in your eyes, please leave them there. If you wipe them away, you give the message that tears are bad.

5. Your presence is important to the reader. You must *stay in the moment*, even though your head and your heart want to pull you away. Listen with your heart on behalf of your friend.

6. As soon as they say their good-bye, immediately offer a hug. You will have a sense of how long the hug should last. Don't rush it. The letter has been a culmination of some very painful work.

7. Remember not to analyze, judge, or criticize. It is not necessarily a good idea to talk about the experience. Talking tends to lead to analysis, judgment, or intellectualizing.

Instructions for the Letter Reader

1. Choose a place that is totally safe for you. Avoid public places.

2. Bring along a box of tissues. There is a high probability that you will experience some strong emotions as you read your letter. Keep the tissues where you can get them. We don't want your listener handing them to you.

3. Before you start reading your letter, close your eyes. Although you have enlisted the help of a listener, your objective is to read the letter to your pet. Get a mental image of the pet you are completing with if you can.

4. Open your eyes. Start reading your letter. You may or may not have an emotional response to your reading. Either way is okay. If you start to choke up, try to talk while you cry. The emotions are contained in the words you have written. Try to push the words up and out of your mouth. Do not swallow your words or your feelings.

5. When you get to the very end, before reading your good-bye sentence, close your eyes, get an image of the pet again, and say your final words. This may be accompanied by many tears. If so, make sure you get the last words spoken, *especially the good-bye.*

6. Remember, you are saying good-bye to the pain; you are saying good-bye to any unfinished business. You are *not* saying good-bye to the fond memories. You are *not* saying good-bye to your spiritual beliefs. Say good-bye to the emotional incompleteness. Say good-bye to the pain, isolation, and confusion. Say good-bye to the physical relationship that you had but that has now ended. Say good-bye and then let it be okay that you cry and let it all out. Also, let it be okay if you do not cry. It is essential that you say good-bye, or you will probably remain incomplete.

7. As soon as you finish, ask your listener for a hug. You might want and need the hug to be quite long. Don't cut it short. You may find yourself sobbing for a while. Let

that be okay with you. You probably have been holding on to the pain for a while. Don't rush the feelings.

WHAT DOES COMPLETION MEAN?

Having taken all of the actions and having read your letter, you are 100 percent complete in your relationship with your pet that died. Completion means that you have discovered and communicated what was unfinished for you in all aspects of the relationship that you have remembered up to this moment. It does not mean that you will never be sad again, any more than you will never be happy again. Completion allows a full range of human emotions attached to your memory of your pet. It means that you don't have to go over the same things again and again. It also means that you don't have to avoid thinking or talking about your pet because you are afraid of what you may feel.

In your day-to-day life, there will be many reminders of your pet. Your moment-to-moment thoughts and feelings will come with emotions attached. Some of your feelings will be happy, fond, and joyful. Some will be negative, sad, and uncomfortable. This is normal. Do not fight it—just allow it. *If you allow negative feelings to occur without resistance, they will pass.* If you try to hide or bury them, they may become painful.

We suggest that you process every feeling in the moment you have it. But what does this mean and how do you do it? In simple terms, that means saying your feeling out loud, and as often as possible with a living witness. For example, when a memory of your pet hits your heart and your response is sad, you'd say, "I just had a feeling about Buda, and in that moment I missed him very much." Notice that instead of saying, "I just had a feeling and I'm depressed," we said, "I had a feeling and *in that moment*

I missed him." Too many people turn a feeling into an all-day event by using overly large time periods to describe their feelings. Feelings are fleeting and will come and go if you don't trap them with incorrect language.

If you are alone when you have a sad or painful feeling, it's okay to say how you feel out loud, even though there's no living witness. It's also okay to say the positive thoughts and feelings you have as you adapt to your life without the pet that died. If you've been alone most of a day without someone to tell those moment-to-moment feelings to, when you get together with your mate or friends later, make a simple statement about your day. It might sound like this: "I had a lot of feelings today, missing Buda sometimes; laughing at how silly he could be other times. I just wanted to share that with you, thanks."

Notice how we phrased that as a statement of what happened, not as an attempt to get into the sadness or pain all over again. Also, your comment can include some positive or happy thoughts you had during the day. Because of the work you did in this book, you will be able to acknowledge the feelings you have, in the moment you have them, and to share them when and where possible. This will help you adapt to the new reality of your life without the pet that died. It means that you don't forget the pet, but you keep the fond memories. The pain will diminish as the result of staying current with your feelings.

However, sometimes there have been very graphic endings to our pets' lives, which leave us with some horrible images that can hit us pretty hard at any time. One of the problems with those recurring images is that they can make us fearful of thinking about our pet that died and limit our access to the fond memories we have of them.

Here's something you can do to help get unstuck from one of those painful images.

STUCK ON A PAINFUL IMAGE

One of the most painful of all experiences is to have your pet die violently. You may have seen the accident or the aftermath. You may have seen photos of the scene, or you may only have the pictures your imagination has conjured up. In any event, for many people the imagery seems constant and as if it will never cease. Some of you may have equally disturbing images of your pet's final hours, days, or weeks as they struggled through a terminal illness.

Most people, in trying to help a friend, will tell them not to think about those images. That is very nearly impossible. We think it is more helpful to acknowledge that the images and pictures are indeed horrible and painful. We also believe that the griever needs to be gently reminded that they have many thousands of other images of their relationship with their pet.

We do not all get to go "gently into that good night," as poetry would have it. A grieving pet owner might tell us of her pet's final night at the clinic, with vivid details. Our response is to say, "What a horrible final picture that is for you." Then we ask, "Do you remember the first time you ever saw your pet?" She says yes, and we say, "Tell us what you remember of that first meeting." And when she does, there's almost always a joy in her voice as the images and pictures of that first meeting come back into her mind and heart.

We all have tens of thousands of images of our loved ones. Some of the images are wonderful and happy. Some are negative and sad. Sometimes the final ones are very painful, as when violence or disease have altered how our pet looked. It is unrealistic to tell someone not to remember what they saw or imagined. By acknowledging the discomfort of the final, unpleasant pictures, we allow the remembering of all the other pictures. Each time the ending pictures crop up, they must be acknowledged.

Acknowledging the painful pictures and remembering others does not deny or minimize the painful ones. When a griever is allowed and encouraged to state what they are experiencing, the painful pictures subside more quickly. This leaves more room for the review of the entire relationship, not just the ending.

NEW DISCOVERIES—PS LETTERS

Sometime after Buda died, Russell and Alice got a new dog whose name is Baxter. He is also a magnificent Hungarian Vizsla, while being totally different in personality from Buda.

You may recall in Russell's letter to Buda that he had always wanted to take Buda to the beach but never got around to it. Within a few weeks of getting Baxter, Russell made a trip down to the legal off-leash dog beach in Huntington Beach, California. As he watched Baxter romping joyfully in the surf and chasing sandpipers at the water line, he felt himself well up with tears. As you can probably imagine, he knew exactly what they were about.

As soon as he got home, he sat down and wrote the following PS letter to Buda:

Dear Buda,

I took Baxter to Huntington Dog Beach today. Even as we drove there I knew it would be emotional for me, and it was very emotional. I thought about you a lot and how much fun you would have had. Buda, I'm sorry that we never got to do this together.

I love you,

I miss you,

Good-bye, Buda.

There was one more action necessary for Russell to be totally complete with the event. The next morning at the office, he asked John to listen while he read the PS letter out loud. After reading the letter, Russell got a hug from John. Russell had created a completed communication by having a living person hear the words he wrote. Just as we have instructed you in the completion process, we do the same.

As you make new discoveries, it doesn't make sense to push them away. It makes more sense to write them down, convert them into recovery categories and then into completion letter form, and read the letter to someone you trust. Each new discovery needs to be completed and verbalized. These actions make room for the next piece to float up to the surface. Most important, staying current by processing all your feelings as soon as possible allows you access to fond memories, rather than being afraid to think about your pet that died because you think it would be too painful.

SADNESS AND JOY ARE
PART OF YOUR MEMORIES

One of the goals of the actions you've taken using this book is to help you feel emotionally complete in your relationship with your pet that died. But it is not intended that you stop having feelings about that pet. We don't want you to stop having feelings, because that would indicate that somehow you've forgotten your pet, which isn't possible.

There will be reminders of your pet everywhere—in your home, in your yard, and everywhere you went with your pet. When you drive by the vet's clinic you'll be reminded. There will be all manner of stimulus that remind you of your pet, and which may cause you to have a momentary feeling of joy or sadness or both. Part of the ongoing legacy of the relationship is to have memories and feelings of the deep bond you had with your pet.

OTHER LETTER EXAMPLES

Over the years we've been privileged to see many of the completion letters people have written to their pets that died. They are all perfect, but this one struck a special chord in us because of the way it demonstrates the emotional power of the human–animal bond. A cowboy who worked on ranches in Texas wrote this letter. It's not as eloquent as some we've seen, but make no mistake, it's just as emotional. The man who wrote it came to one of our seminars wearing a cowboy hat and boots, and wearing his heart on his sleeve. He was tougher than nails but as heartbroken as anyone we've ever met.

Dear Boy,

I guess I have to call you boy, because in the 12 years you hung around, I never gave you a name. I either called you boy, or fleabag, or mutt, or something like that.

Don't know that I ever really liked you—heck, I don't know that you liked me. I think the only reasons you stayed around were because I fed you and because you could sneak in and lay down next to me when it was cold.

You were a scrawny fleabag of a mutt, and I don't know how I ever let you near me in the first place, I didn't need no dog, anyway. You were just there and since I never could figure out how to get rid of you, it got more and more like you belonged there, so I just let you stay.

Like I said, I'm not saying that I liked you or nothing like that. Just that I sort of got used to you. And I got used to talking at you like you could understand. Probably you were just a dumb old dog, but maybe I am too, because I talked to you all the time. There were times when I actually thought that you understood what I was saying, but I know that's crazy—you couldn't really understand words.

And I remember that I'd tell you some long-winded story, and you'd sit there like I was saying something really important and then you'd put your head on my leg and go to sleep. I guess my stories could put a fellow to sleep, but at least you listened 'til I'd told the whole story. Not everybody would do that, so thanks for listening.

I know I was sometimes mean to you, though I never did hit you or nothing. But I could be a cranky old fool sometimes, so I'm sorry if I said some mean things to you. Not that you really could understand, but I think you knew to give me some room, when my voice got all nasty and all. Sorry pal, I just had to get it out of me, and you were the only one around.

Oh, and the man here says that I need to forgive you for the times you took off and nearly gave me a heart attack, especially when we were in the city where you could get hurt. I could always trust you out in the country, you knew how to be out there, but you weren't very smart about cars. I sure wanted to wring your scrawny neck a few times for the fact that you nearly got yourself killed, but I forgive you.

What the heck was I supposed to do without you, you fool dog? So here I am anyway and you're gone and, darned if I don't miss you. Don't make sense, I never wanted you and now I miss you. And that darned vet, giving me the idea that I should be with you when he gave you the shot that put you away. I didn't want him to see me cry, but he did. Until then, in the past 12 years, you were the only one who ever saw me cry. Even then you only saw me cry twice, once when I heard my momma had died, and the other time when I heard that my little brother landed up in jail.

Both times you got up and licked my face, with your dog breath and all, like you knew I was really upset. I never got to tell anyone about that, 'til today. Anyhow, thanks for looking after this crusty old loner of a cowboy. I guess you're the closest I've ever felt to the thing they call love.
Good-bye, Boy

This next letter is not exactly an example of a completion letter. It is an e-mail that Russell sent to John the morning after he got back from the vet's office on the last day of Buda's life. We think it a fitting way to end this chapter.

BUDA'S LAST HUNT

Dear John,
    Early this morning I took Buda to the park over at Hazeltine, the one he and I had gone to nearly every day for years.
    Although he was very ill, he knew where we were when we drove into the parking lot and perked up.
    God was watching, for sure, because there were doves everywhere.
    I took his leash off and Buda went into full hunting mode—every instinct and ounce of adrenaline on overdrive. He stalked and pointed and gave chase.
    Blessedly, Alice had made me go out and buy one of those instant cameras late last night, so I managed to catch Buda doing exactly what he was born to do.
    After a while, we started back to the front end of the park where Alice was going to meet us.
    Just as we neared the area, I spotted a squirrel flitting from tree to tree and I pointed it out to Buda (isn't he supposed to be the pointer?). He saw it and took off and treed it.

With what little strength was left in his body, he leapt and twisted trying to reach it like he always did and then barked to try to scare it down. Of course it just chirped and mocked Buda from on high.

Buda then sat down in that military posture of his and cocked his head up and he and the squirrel played eye-chess for ten minutes. People passing by stopped to watch—just like the old days.

I ran out of tissues.

Alice arrived a few minutes later. By then, Buda had spotted up on another squirrel on a lower branch, which was staring back at him. We watched this nature documentary and then God got into the act again.

The squirrel—possibly suicidal—started down the trunk of the tree and went all the way to the ground. Buda was no more than 6 feet from him. To the best of my knowledge, Buda had never caught a squirrel. I made an instant decision that this might be his last chance. I decided to let nature take its course.

Buda gave chase, but the squirrel managed to get under a car in the parking lot.

That was Buda's last hunt.

I helped Buda into my car and we drove to the vet's office. Several friends joined us there. The vet and the tech all cried along with us. Right up to the end Buda brought out the humanness in people.

I am positive that the squirrels in heaven have their own Homeland Security and that they raised the code to the highest alert level at about 9:20 a.m. this morning.

No more words, for now.

Russell

9

MORE TO DO? MAYBE!

As you've been reading this book and taking the actions it outlines, we're sure you've become aware that you may need to review and graph some other relationships with pets that have graced your life and then write completion letters to them.

Now that you know how to do it, there's nothing to stop you. The process is much quicker the second time through. You don't have to go all the way back to the beginning and create a new Pet Loss History Graph. After you choose which pet to work on next, you can start with the relationship graph, convert it into the recovery categories, and then write your completion letter.

When you have written your completion letter, you will again have to find a safe listener. If you had a good experience with the listener who sat for your first letter reading, it's a good idea to ask that person to sit for you again. Remember to find a safe place, remind him of the guidelines, and read your letter. Oh, and have tissues handy.

In this follow-up work, some people write more than one graph and letter to different pets that have been important in their lives. It's okay to read more than one letter when you have your listener available, but make sure to have a gap in time between each reading. You want to honor the unique relationship with each pet by not reading the letters too closely together. Generally we don't recommend reading more than two letters in a day. If you have more than two, get together again a few days later if possible.

Loss is inevitable, but now that you have this toolkit of the Grief Recovery Method actions, you can approach new relationships with less fear of the feelings you might have in the future if that pet dies. We know that many people never get another pet because of that fear. By doing that, they rob themselves—and a potential pet—of the loving companionship they could have together.

READY FOR ANOTHER PET?

The preceding chapters of this book were devoted to the emotional completion that can help you move forward in your life after the death of your cherished animal companion. With that completion you'll be better equipped to decide if and when you want to get another pet. You will know that you are not "replacing the loss" but are establishing a new and valuable relationship with a different being. You will also know that you are not using the new pet to distract yourself from feelings you have about the pet that died.

The amount of time between the death of your pet and when you get another is unique to each of us. There is no rule, and not even a general guideline, that would fit all of us. When Buda died, Russell and Alice were emotionally devastated. But even as they grieved, they each took the actions of the Grief Recovery Method that helped them feel emotionally complete with the things that did and didn't happen with Buda. Russell recalls that as he adapted to the new reality of life without Buda, the amount of crying and missing Buda diminished.

Buda died in early April of 2005. One day in June, Russell found himself looking at online Vizsla rescue sites. When he got home that night, he told Alice. She asked him if he felt ready. He said, "I asked myself that same question today, because I had gone to that Vizsla site. I realized that my heart was ready, that's why I was looking."

The key for Russell and Alice wasn't the amount of time that elapsed after Buda had died, it was the work that each of them had done to help themselves feel emotionally complete that allowed them to decide they wanted another pet. The result was Baxter, also a magnificent Vizsla, who was able to establish his own identity and become a member of their family without replacing or being compared to Buda.

CLEANUP WORK

After you take the actions of completion, you will gain a new perspective. Things look different because you have changed on the inside. Completing your relationship with your pet that died brought about this change. Since the inside has changed, it will now be necessary to look at the outside. You'll want to adjust your environment to reflect this new inside perspective on the loss.

The first step in your cleanup work will be to look at outside reminders of the loss. Some grieving pet owners hold on to everything that represents the pet that died. That is called enshrinement. Often, people hold on to all these things when they are emotionally incomplete with the loss.

Since you have taken the actions of emotional completion, you will not need to hold on to all of the objects that represent your pet. Some of the objects won't seem to fit with your new perspective; these are the ones you'll want to dispose of. It is normal to want to keep some things and not be sure about others.

Well-intended friends may have advised you to just get rid of it all—bedding, cages, crates, collars, leashes, saddles, bridles, toys, mementos—everything. But you may not want to get rid of it all, and it isn't a good idea for most grieving pet owners. We've heard too many stories of people who followed that guidance, threw everything away, and then regretted it when they wanted or needed a physical reminder of their pet.

Before you rush out and throw everything away, let's make a plan that will work. *When possible never do any of these chores alone.*

THE ABC PLAN—WHAT TO DO WITH YOUR PET'S STUFF

One of the most painful tasks for grieving pet owners is deciding what to keep and what to discard. One of the reasons it's so difficult is because each object is an emotional reminder of your pet that died. One good approach has been called the ABC Plan. This approach can be used for all of the things associated with your pet. It has also been lovingly referred to as the Pile Plan. You'll see why as we go along.

Before you start taking this action, if possible, make sure you have someone you trust with you. There is a high probability that sorting through all the things related to your pet will generate some emotions in you. Ask that person to allow you to tell your memories with emotions attached, without judgment or analysis.

The objective is to wind up with what you want to keep without keeping things you don't need or want. So, take all the objects and put them in the living room. Go through them one at a time. If you want to talk about a memory that any of the articles stimulates for you, please do so with the person helping you. You will than put each item into one of three piles. The piles should be grouped as follows:

Pile A contains the things that you are certain you want to keep.

Pile B contains the things that you are certain you want to dispose of; things to sell; things to give away—possibly to pet-support organizations.

Pile C contains all those things that you're not sure about yet. If there is any doubt at all about which pile an item goes in, it goes in Pile C.

You are not in a race. You're employing a clear plan that works. As you stand in the room looking at all the items, it may dawn on you why some people refer to this as the Pile Plan. Dispose of the piles as follows:

Pile A goes wherever you want to keep those things, possibly in an area you associate with your pet.

Pile B is given to individuals, organizations, and so forth.

Pile C goes into bags and boxes and to the garage in an area where you can get at it easily.

When you're done, congratulate yourself and thank your friend.

One month later, bring all the Pile C bags and boxes back into the living room and work the plan all over again. Once again, never alone! Your new Pile A is for the things you find that you definitely want to keep. Pile B is for those things you are now sure you want to discard. Everything else is Pile C and goes back into the bags and boxes, and into the garage for another month.

Doing this task one more time should accomplish your goal of keeping what you want to keep and not retaining things that you don't need. If necessary, do it all over again in three months. Eventually you will be done.

PASSING ON BUDA'S LEGACY

Russell recalls having done the Pile Plan after Buda died. Of course, there were leashes, and collars, and food bowls, and many other things. It's sometimes surprising to see how much stuff you've collected over the years. The first time through, Russell experienced a lot of emotion, talking about Buda and remembering when and why he'd acquired some of the things he'd assembled in the living room. Because of the emotional attachment, Russell didn't throw away a lot of those things the first time. But the C pile, with things that he would look at again and decide about later, was a couple of big bags full. They went into the garage.

The second go-through was less emotional, and by then, Russell had a clearer sense of what to keep and what to discard. Some of those objects later became part of Baxter's life and routines and now are part of a legacy passed from Buda to Baxter. Russell loves the reminders of Buda, which help create a constant sense of positive connection.

Russell also realizes that just knowing to take the actions of the ABC Plan probably saved him a lot of grief; he might have thrown away a lot of stuff that he would have regretted.

DEALING WITH SPECIAL DATES

Even after all the work you've done, there are still going to be certain reminders that have the potential for making you feel sad and miss your pet. This is not only because of the love you shared with your pet, but also because of all the familiar routines and habits you established with your pet. Memories and feelings can be provoked by special dates or by objects or photos, or by anything and everything you see, touch, or hear. You may also find yourself having a lot of feelings about your pet that died, without being able to trace it to a specific date, event, or object. If that happens, please understand that it is totally normal. Let it be okay with you.

For many people, one of the by-products of doing the work in this book is to have more conscious awareness of their emotions. Your relationship with your pet, along with your emotional response to his death, may have awakened your capacity to experience and express your feelings. If that is true for you, you might write a PS letter thanking your pet for your newfound connection to your emotions.

WE CONGRATULATE YOU!

Throughout this book we've tried to be as supportive and encouraging as possible. We have congratulated you several times along the way for your courage and willingness to take the actions we outlined. Now we want to thank you for trusting us to guide you in those actions.

10

CONCLUSIONARY RITUALS

The preceding chapters of this book were devoted to the emotional completion that can help you move forward in your life after the death of your cherished animal companion. In addition to dealing with your emotions, there are some practical matters related to end-of-life issues that also must be addressed. Although it may have been a while since your pet died, we want to give you some valuable guidance about conclusionary rituals and burials which may come in handy for you at a later date, or on behalf of friends or family.

Over the many years we've been helping grieving people, we've come into contact with a tremendous number of funeral directors and cemeterians, all of whom are in the trenches with grieving people in the days immediately following the death of someone meaningful to them. We've also had the privilege of meeting and knowing some very special people who operate facilities that provide pet funerals and burials. They are unique in their concern for the dignified handling of the pet's remains, and they are exceptionally aware of the emotions of the people who are grieving the deaths of their pets.

As you will read in this chapter, the memorializing of our pets is ancient, going back thousands of years. Effective rituals—in which we remember and honor the pets we love—enhance the emotional completion outlined in this book.

INTRODUCING DEREK COOKE AND
ABBEY GLEN PET MEMORIAL PARK

We are thrilled to introduce you to our great friend Derek Cooke. Derek is one of the cofounders of Abbey Glen Pet Memorial Park and a major force in changing the landscape of awareness and emotional well-being on behalf of grieving pet owners everywhere. We have been honored to know him for many years. And we are even more honored now that he has contributed his personal and professional story to this book. We'll let him tell you how and why he came to devote his life to the care and concern of people and the animals they love.

DEREK COOKE—HOW I ARRIVED
IN THE PET CEMETERY BUSINESS

My name is Derek Cooke, and in order to put myself into this picture, I have to give you a little family history. My grandmother, widowed with a young child, decided the best chance for the boy was to be raised by a foster family. The boy was my father, and the family who raised him owned and operated a boarding kennel in Closter, New Jersey. Those early years my father spent living and working with pets became the foundation for his love of animals.

After high school, he served as a Marine Corps drill instructor at Paris Island, South Carolina. After his discharge, he married my beautiful mother, earned his college degree, and settled into a job with a large corporation. I came along in the fall of 1960, and the first of my two younger brothers came three years later. By that time, Dad had decided that working a nine-to-five job for a big company was not for him. In 1965, with a wife and two toddlers in tow, he decided to leave his job. He'd heard of an old boarding kennel that was for sale in Warren, New Jersey, and he figured he could apply what he'd learned as a lad working at the kennel to revive that business.

We settled into our new rural home, and Dad devoted his time and energy to rebuilding the kennel business. My formative years were spent attending school and working with my two younger brothers at our boarding facility, where we provided loving care for pets when their owners were out of town. Similar to my father's experience, I spent a great deal of my childhood living and working with pets, which served as the beginning of my lifelong, loving connection to animals.

Over the years, my father developed long-term, personal relationships with many of his clients. Inevitably, our phone would ring at all hours of the day or night. Frequently, one of those clients—distraught over the death of their pet—would call for advice on what to do.

As these calls continued over time, my father became increasingly frustrated with his inability to provide real assistance to those hurting people. He realized there was a major gap in the services we provided. In 1976, he erected a modest building on the side of the kennel property to house a small cremation chamber. From that point on, when someone whose pet had died called him, he had the resources to help.

It didn't take long for awareness of our cremation chamber to spread, and calls for assistance increased. Soon, other people, spurred by their personal or religious beliefs, expressed a desire for a place to bury their pets, as opposed to cremation. With a continued interest in meeting the needs of grieving pet owners, my father began to look for land. He spent the next few years trying to buy land suitable for burial grounds, but his bids were rejected by the local township committees and zoning boards. Ultimately, he had to travel to the northern-most reaches of the state, to the small farming community of Lafayette, New Jersey. Surprisingly, that community gave him permission to develop an abandoned local farm into a cemetery for pets.

Like my dad, I had also gone into the Marine Corps. About the time Dad found the Lafayette property, I was near the end of my active duty tour and my two brothers were finishing their college careers. Ultimately, we all came together to develop that farm in northern New Jersey into a special place to memorialize the unique relationships between man and animal. We named it the Abbey Glen Pet Memorial Park and Home for Pet Funerals.

Many years later, our world continues to revolve around caring for animal companions. My family and I still operate the Roxdane Kennels Pet Care Center in Warren, New Jersey, and we provide exclusive burial and cremation services for beloved pets at the Abbey Glen Pet Memorial Park in Lafayette, New Jersey. That's almost fifty years of caring for pets in one way or another.

MEMORIAL TRIBUTE TO
ANIMAL COMPANIONS IS NOT NEW

Many cultures throughout history have paid tribute to their animals by burying them in a respectful manner:

- **Egypt:** The ancient Egyptians mummified and buried cats, which they considered deities.
- **Israel:** The largest dog cemetery in the ancient world was discovered at the Ashkelon National Park in Ashkelon, Israel.
- **Great Britain:** Hyde Park was the site of an informal pet cemetery between 1881 and 1903 in the gatekeeper's garden.
- **France:** Cimetière des Chiens in Asnières-sur-Seine in Paris is an elaborate, sculpted pet cemetery believed to be one of the first public zoological necropolises, dating from 1899.

- **Peru:** Archaeologists have uncovered more than forty mummified dogs in a thousand-year-old pet cemetery south of Lima.
- **China:** Archeologists have found an ancient dog cemetery in Beijing with tombstones of marble, ivory, and silver.

CHANGING TIMES

As the list above shows, memorializing an animal companion's life is a custom that has been evidenced throughout history, yet it is clear that over time something has shifted that limits our expression of the affection we have for our pets. I'm not sure when or why our modern culture became so self-conscious about the normal and natural emotions connected to the deaths of our pets, but I do know that some of the time-honored practices of memorializing the companions with whom we've shared our lives have been stifled.

During my early years of helping pet owners with the deaths of their pets, I witnessed a period when these matters needed to be handled discreetly and behind closed doors for fear of social ridicule. Now, I am happy to report that the tide is turning, and many people can at least express sympathy for those who experience the death of a cherished pet. That expression helps, but there's still a long way to go so that grieving pet owners no longer need fear being judged for their sadness.

Evidence of Change

I began attending veterinary seminars and conventions as an exhibitor in the early 1980s. I would stand in the exhibit hall at conventions surrounded by other exhibitors marketing surgical devices, x-ray equipment, prescription pet foods, or insurance policies. Our booth displayed a pet casket, a sampling of cremation urns, and a few enlarged pictures of our beautiful cemetery grounds.

Veterinarians and their hospital staff roamed the aisles, stopping to chat with each exhibitor and examining their wares. But when they got near our booth and saw our display, there was a moment of realization. With it came a change in facial expression, and a shift in the direction of travel. It was particularly discouraging to me at the time, because these were the professionals whom I had revered growing up.

The good news is that we no longer encounter this behavior. In fact, today's generation of veterinary healthcare professionals value the role of memorial service providers, and they have invited us into their practices as a partnered service provider.

THE PURPOSE AND VALUE OF A CONTEMPORARY PET CEMETERY

In my experience, there are two primary values that can and should be afforded by a well-established professionally operated pet cemetery:

1. *A safe environment.* Society is now more accepting of the grief and emotional distress caused by the death of a pet. However, people's individual reactions can still be unpredictable. As a result, most grieving pet owners instinctively restrain themselves from openly expressing their emotions. A sincere, professional staff at a pet cemetery will quickly create a safe environment where even the most cautious grievers will feel safe to express themselves honestly. That is a tremendous relief for someone, who, up to that point, has felt they had to keep it all in.

2. *A therapeutic process.* Each of my three Rottweilers died
   at various ages and at different points in time over the
   past ten years. With each death, I found myself drawn to
   perform the practical actions that our firm typically does
   to help our clients. I drove each one to the cremation
   chamber at the pet cemetery and placed the body into
   the chamber. I waited for the cremation to be complete;
   then I put the ashes into an urn that displayed their picture. I said my "I love you" and "good-bye." ***My companions were safe.***

Note: Before taking my pets to the crematorium, I took the Grief
Recovery Method actions, exactly the same ones as laid out in this
book. Although still saddened by each death, I felt as emotionally
complete as possible.

AND SAFETY WHEN MY MOTHER DIED

I also want to tell you that my mother died a few years ago at
the age of seventy-two, following a long and graceful battle
with breast cancer. Following long-held funerary traditions, the
women of our family personally took care of the cosmetology
and dressed my mother's body in preparation for the memorial
and funeral. The men placed her in the casket and carried it to
the living room so that we could have a private viewing for family
and close friends.

The next day we asked a licensed funeral director to transport
her body to the local cemetery where her mausoleum space had
been prepared next to her parents. We placed her casket into the
hearse and rode to the cemetery with her. My father and brothers
and I carried the casket from the car to the open crypt. We each

took a moment to say a few last words and then placed her inside, ourselves. The cemetery staff permanently affixed the cover to the crypt and it was done. ***My mother was safe.***

ALL RELATIONSHIPS ARE UNIQUE— NO COMPARISONS AND NO EXCEPTIONS

With my mother and with my pets that died, I had a sense of "completion." The completion was a combination of the personal Grief Recovery Method work I'd done on each relationship, the communications I had about them with my family, and ensuring that their bodies were safe and where I could visit them as and when needed.

I do not feel that I'm doing a disservice to the memory of my mother by talking about my reaction to her death along with my reaction to the deaths of my dogs. Each of those relationships was unique and individual, and each needed to be grieved and completed for what they were. Also equal was my need to make sure their respective bodies were handled with dignity along the way.

I am not comparing the death of my mother to the deaths of my dogs; nor am I comparing the death of any of the animals to the others. The point I want to make in each situation is that I achieved physical closure by taking care of the bodies, and emotional completion by using the Grief Recovery Method to take care of my heart. I am comforted by the knowledge that each of my loved ones was laid to rest in a respectful manner and that I had seen to it personally and had participated in the process all the way to the end.

Not everyone has the knowledge and willingness to do what I did. But the caring and professional staff of a pet cemetery or crematory can fulfill its most valued purpose by providing a grieving individual with the opportunity to define and participate in the process of laying their cherished companion to rest. They can also help by normalizing the grief, creating a safe environment in which to express that grief, and by serving as a guide through the process.

PERMANENT RE-LOCATABLE GRIEF RECOVERY MONUMENT

My personal experience, coupled with my connection to thousands of grieving pet owners over the years, indicates that having a gravesite to visit can be a great comfort. An ongoing benefit of having a burial site in a pet cemetery, or a niche in a columbarium, is that it provides a permanent re-locatable grief recovery monument that you and others can visit. It can be emotionally valuable to take your children or grandchildren and tell them about some of the pets that graced your life before they were born.

PRACTICAL CHOICES TO KNOW WHEN YOUR PET DIES

A pet cemetery-crematory can provide convenient access to memorial products and services that may be needed or desired as components of a funeral:

- A headstone to mark the burial site, whether at a cemetery or at home in the backyard.
- A selection of caskets and/or urns to choose from.
- Services to transport a pet's body to the cemetery or crematory.

If the memorial service provider is a pet cemetery that also offers cremation, then pet owners have three options from which to choose:

- **Burial in the cemetery:** affording the pet owner a permanent place to go.
- **Individual cremation:** with the individual pet's ashes returned to the pet owner. This option typically affords the pet owner an urn keepsake to serve as a memorial or the ability to scatter their pet's ashes in a place of their own choosing.
- **Group or communal cremation:** one of the methods of ash disposition depending upon the service provider. A pet cemetery that also offers cremation will often memorialize communal cremains in a section of their cemetery, creating a permanent re-locatable place to go.

BE CAREFUL, YOU MAY
NOT BE THINKING CLEARLY

We know that on that fateful day at the vet's office, when presented with choices about the disposition of your pet's remains, you may not be thinking clearly. If you can, bring someone along with you that you trust, someone who can help you with the decisions that need to be made at that time. We caution you by relating the following scenario that we have observed many times over the years:

A pet dies at a veterinary facility. In an effort to be helpful, a veterinarian may try to save a distraught client from further details and decisions by determining a method of disposition for them. Or, if presented with the details, the distraught client may not fully comprehend or digest the information and unwittingly sign for group cremation. It may take a few days or weeks after

the death, but often the pet owner will discover what has actually occurred relative to their pet's disposition. Thinking more
clearly at this point, they may realize that group cremation was
not what they wanted for their pet, but it is too late. When that
happens, the effects of not having the individual remains of their
pet can be a crushing disappointment. Even a special section of
the pet cemetery, where group cremains are memorialized, may
be insufficient comfort for a devastated pet owner.

ABBEY GLEN CREATED A
PERSONALIZED SOLUTION

Having heard that scenario many times, we realized that we had to
do something to help those people who were having such a hard
time with what had happened. At Abbey Glen, we erected two
large marble and bronze memorials in the section where group
cremains are memorialized. We call these "Gift of Love" memorials. We offer pet owners the opportunity to purchase a bronze
plate with their pet's name, family name, year of birth, and year
of death. The finished plate is then permanently mounted on the
much larger Gift of Love memorial. This creates a personalized
memorial and place to go. This is the best we have been able to do
for pet owners who found themselves in this position because they
hadn't been given the full range of options at the time their pet
died, or hadn't understood what was being offered.

AS WITH ALL THINGS, BE DILIGENT

There's no shortage of pet cemeteries and crematories these days.
However, like anything else, it takes due diligence to identify a
good one. Here are some helpful suggestions:

- Visit the cemetery or crematory.
- Try to visit more than one so you can make a comparison.
- Don't trust pictures on the Internet.
- Don't go exclusively on the recommendation of a veterinarian. Most veterinarians are too busy running their practices to personally visit the facilities to which they refer.
- Meet with the staff to see if they are indeed professional, compassionate, and attentive.
- Ask if you are able to see and/or participate in every aspect of either a burial or cremation service. Nothing should need to occur behind closed doors or out of your view.
- Make sure the pet cemetery land is "deed restricted." This ensures that the land is dedicated for permanent use as a pet cemetery, regardless of who owns it.
- A dedicated pet cemetery should have a perpetual or permanent care fund. You will be asked to make an irrevocable payment into the fund, the principal of which may not be touched. The interest generated by the principal is used to ensure the continued care and maintenance of the cemetery.

In closing our section of this wonderful book, on behalf of my family and the extended Abbey Glen family, I want to thank all the pet owners who have trusted us with the final disposition of the pets they love. I also want to thank John, Russell, and Cole and the Grief Recovery Method team around the world for the work they do every day in helping grieving people.

BRITAIN—A NATION OF ANIMAL LOVERS FINDING ITS EMOTIONAL VOICE

This is a special section from Nick Ricketts, chairman of the Association of Private Pet Cemeteries and Crematoria—Great Britain (http://www.appcc.org.uk/). Carole Batchelor, the director of the Grief Recovery Method, UK, cowrote this with Nick so that readers in Britain will become aware of what is possible at the end of their pets' lives. As you read it, you'll notice that the guidance matches up to what Derek wrote earlier in the chapter.

In Britain we often describe ourselves as a nation of animal lovers, with about half of all households having at least one pet of some kind. Yet despite this comfortable assertion, almost without exception, the people we talk to who have had a pet die constantly hear, "Don't feel bad, you can get another one."

This is perhaps partly because of the sad generality that we British are so good at burying our feelings and "We don't want to make a fuss." It has only been relatively recently that we have seen growth in the demand for individual pet cremations, pet burials, and pet funerals.

Traditionally, pets were either buried at home or left at the veterinarian's clinic. When we talked to people about the option of leaving the disposal to the veterinarian, they revealed that they generally avoided thinking about it. The subject was taboo, and most of them didn't want to know what the veterinarians did. They felt as if they had no choice but to go along with it.

However, over the past thirty years we have seen an increase in family run pet crematoria, many of which also offer burial options to meet the growing demand from pet owners for a loving and dignified end for their companions. Unfortunately, the majority of the pet owning public are still unaware that such facilities exist here. If they have heard of them, they may not be aware that they are welcome to bring the animal themselves, rather than leave everything to their vet to decide for them. For that reason, and many others, we are pleased to be able to create some awareness in this most necessary book.

Another issue is that many facilities find it difficult to promote themselves because it is still such a taboo topic in this country. Again, being added to this dignified book, which makes the topic of grief so much more within limits than not, we hope to spread the word about what is possible. That way, grieving pet owners can participate in choices that will help them feel more emotionally complete with their pets that have died.

Sadly, we also have a situation where several large "disposal" companies offer veterinary practices lucrative inducements to use their services. Therefore, these practices are very reluctant to give customers the option of going elsewhere. However, if you, the consumer, know of other and better options, you won't have to be limited to that one choice.

The Association of Private Pet Cemeteries & Crematoria

The Association of Private Pet Cemeteries & Crematoria UK (APPCC) was formed twenty-one years ago. Along with other criteria, one of its primary objectives was to give pet owners reassurance about the services they receive. Member firms agree to comply with a Code of Conduct. This code stipulates that all operations carried out should be honest and transparent, thereby giving the assurance that "What is carried out is in accordance with the owners' wishes, and that they are able to verify that this is the case, at each stage of the process."

We always suggest that if you're a pet owner you should do your research, preferably before your pet has died. As with planning human funerals, it's much easier to make decisions when you are not in the midst of deep grief. We know that you don't always have advance notice, but we think it a good idea to spread the word so that if and when an untimely ending occurs, you will at least know what options are available to you. (Yes, we know that all deaths of the pets we love are untimely.)

Not Knowing Adds to the Unresolved Grief

Unresolved grief is often exacerbated by the pain and confusion of not knowing what becomes of the pet's remains. Despite reassurances from the veterinarian's staff, the owner may wonder what really happens. They are afraid to challenge the staff in case their worst fears are confirmed.

Firstly, talk to your vet and find out the details of what, if any, postdeath service is provided. If you are totally happy with what is being offered, that's great; if not, then look around at alternative service providers. An increasing number of funeral directors offer a pet service, although they won't necessarily advertise this. Whether or not you use a funeral director to make the arrangements for you, it is worth checking if the crematorium or cemetery is an APPCC member.

We also suggest a visit to the facility in advance, to satisfy yourself that they can provide you with the service you are looking for. All reputable facilities have reception rooms where you can spend some time with your pet before any process takes place. If you are unable or unwilling to bring your pet yourself, then proper facilities will offer a dignified collection service.

A common concern is whether or not your pet was cremated individually. The APPCC code insists that pet owners should be offered the opportunity to witness their pet being placed in the cremator. Whether or not you take this opportunity is entirely individual—indeed you may not have chosen to have an individual cremation—but if you have, being given the chance to witness the proceeding and reassure yourself may be an important component in your recovery.

Similarly, if you so desire, then you should be offered the option to witness the cremated remains being taken from the plant. The processed ash will be contained in a plastic bag with a label

identifying the contents—name, size of pet, and date of cremation. The bagged ashes may then be placed in a chosen container.

Family-run pet crematoria usually offer a range of ash con-
tainers, according to taste and preference. Urns and caskets are
available for long-term retention, or scatter tubes-pouches if the
pet is to be scattered at a special memorable location.

You should also be given a certificate of cremation and some
sort of identification on the container such as a nameplate. Ad-
ditionally, many facilities offer such options as entries in a book of
remembrance. Extracts from it may often also be available.

The whole process should be such that the bereaved can say
good-bye to their companion, confident that what they expected
to happen did indeed happen.

Our Thanks to the Folks at the Grief Recovery Method

All of us at the Association of Private Pet Cemeteries & Crematoria are honored to be included in this book. We thank our
member firms for caring for and about the pet owners they serve;
and we thank Carole, John, Russell, Cole, and the thousands of
Grief Recovery Method specialists around the world.

ABOUT EMPTY GRAVES AND
LOCAL RULES AND REGULATIONS

There are two more issues that we want to address to conclude
this chapter. The first relates to an article we wrote several years
ago called "America's Empty Graves." In it, we brought up the
very romantic notion of scattering the ashes of people who have
died into the ocean, or releasing them from airplanes. The reason
we wrote the article is because it is estimated that there are more

than one million empty graves in the United States: graves with inscribed head stones or metal markers but with neither a casket, a body, nor even an urn with ashes inside. Most people don't know anything about this strange phenomenon or how it came to be.

What many people discover some time after having released the ashes to the water or to the four winds is that they are missing a crucial element for their ongoing recovery from the death of the person—or pet—that died. The missing piece is a permanent, re-locatable place to go where there is an aspect of the physical being that acts as a tangible reminder of their relationship with the entity who died. Confronted with that absence, more than a million people have purchased gravesites, stones, and markers so they will have a place to go to remember and reflect on someone important to them who died. We don't have a way of getting an accurate statistic on the same phenomenon relative to pets whose ashes were strewn on the water or to the winds, but we'd guess the number is also very high.

KEEP A PORTION OF THE
ASHES TO STAY CONNECTED

Many dying people request that their survivors disperse their ashes in a major body of water or into the four winds. The ideas behind that kind of dispersal may be romantic or spiritual. Although our pets can't make that kind of request, we know a lot of people do that with their pets' cremains for similar reasons. We have no problem with that. But we've had to help many people who did that and later regretted it. Many of them are among the ones who later purchased gravesites when they realized they didn't have a place to go.

When asked by grievers prior to a planned dispersal, we always suggest that they keep at least a small portion of the ashes, so they will have a tangible and permanent re-locatable connection to the pet (or person) they loved.

RULES AND REGULATIONS

Again, we have no problem with scattering the ashes in the water or into the wind or other methods, as long as doing so has meaning and value for the griever. And, to repeat, we strongly urge you to keep a small portion of the ashes in a safe place for future reverence.

Caution: Throughout the United States, Great Britain, and other countries, there are local rules and regulations regarding the scattering of ashes. Please make sure that you don't break any of those laws. With the use of online searches, you can easily find out what, if any, restrictions there might be. Nick at APPCC puts it very well: "It's no good doing your own thing and then having repercussions at a later date!"

IN CLOSING—FROM US TO YOU

Recovery from grief or loss is achieved by a series of small and correct action choices made by the griever. Having had this opportunity to pass along the actions of the Grief Recovery Method as specifically applied to the death of a pet heartens us.

We know that many people will read this book and benefit from what we've written. But we also know that the ultimate benefit is the result of taking the actions the book outlines. We are honored that you have read the book.

Unresolved grief is cumulative and cumulatively negative. The longer you wait to do the work, the more fearful you will become.

If you have read the book, but haven't yet taken the actions, we strongly encourage you to make a commitment to yourself to take the actions—very soon. Please don't allow the experience of reading and understanding to lull you into the idea that you are complete. Completion is the result of action. As always, you have our support and our respect for your courage and willingness.

John W. James
Russell Friedman
Cole James

The Grief Recovery Method®
Contact information for any of our programs, worldwide.

In the United States or Canada:
Contact us at: www.griefrecoverymethod.com
Email: info@griefrecoverymethod.com
Tel: From within the US: 800-334-7606
From Outside the US: 818-907-9600

In the United Kingdom:
Contact **Carole Batchelor**
www.griefrecoverymethod.co.uk/
Email: help@griefrecoverymethod.co.uk
Tel: 01234 862218

In Mexico and Latin America:
Contact **Arturo Albin** or **Alejandra Rivero**
metodogriefrecovery.com/
info@metodogriefrecovery.com
Para informes o inscripciones, llámanos México DF 52 (55) 5245-1658
En Estados Unidos en Español (805) 910-4511

In Sweden and throughout Scandinavia:
Contact **Anders Magnusson**
Svenska Institutet för Sorgbearbetning: www.sorg.se
Email: info@sorg.se
Tegnérgatan 24   -   113 59 Stockholm
Tfn: 08-33 50 40 Fax: 08-33 50 46

In Australia:
Contact **Amanda Lambros**
www.griefrecoverymethod.com.au/
Email: info@griefrecoverymethod.com.au
1-800-763-538

We are training and adding other partners around the globe.
Please check: www.griefrecoverymethod.com
from time to time to see our latest international additions.